SIDMOUTI

A History
JACOBS LADDER to the ALMA BRIDGE

Compiled by
John Ankins and Daughter, Margaret Taylor

Typesetting by A. & P. Tully
South West Typesetting Sidmouth

Printed by Westprint
Clyst Court
Blackmore Road
Hill Barton Business Park
Clyst St. Mary
Exeter

First Published in 2007 by John Ankins

ISBN 0 9538021 - 4 - 0

CHAPTERS

INTRODUCTION

W Collins, R.N. Published by J & L Arch. February 1821.

"Sidmouth is a small seaport and market town on the coast of Devonshire. It is situated at the mouth of a narrow valley, through which the little river Sid flows towards the ocean, where it is lost in the pebbles on the beach. It was once a commodious harbour; but has been so choked up with sand and pebbles, that pleasure boats and fishing-smacks are the only vessels which now venture to approach the shore. Its population and buildings have, however, lately increased, from its having become a favourite place for sea bathing and summer recreation, for which it now possesses all the necessary conveniences and accommodations to promote its comforts and pleasures. The adjacent country presents delightful prospects, and the scenery on the coast from Sidmouth to Seaton, is considered as the finest on the southern coast of Devonshire." *

* A quotation from Maton's Observations, Vol. 1. 1821.

19th CENTURY IMAGES OF SIDMOUTH SEA FRONT

Lithograph by George Rowe. 1826.

Eastern View, from Wallis's Library, Sidmouth 1829.

George Rowe. 1826   Published by J. Wallis, Maritime Library.

View of Sidmouth 1828.

3

The Royal York Hotel and Library, Sidmouth.   W. H. Bartlett. 1829.

Post Card Early 1900.

A BRIEF HISTORY

The weather affects the visitor, locals and trade, and the cost to protect the town. Locals and visitors say "Sidmouth never changes". The town and seafront have not gone down the way other seaside places have

There have been Punch and Judy shows on the beach in the past, and in 1900 Mr. Spencer gave children donkey rides on the sands in the summer. The donkeys were stabled in the cellars of the Bedford Hotel. Out of the holiday season they went to Branscombe to bring in the early local potatoes, which were grown on the cliffs.

Sidmouth has, in most years, held a Regatta for one week in August. The first reference I have found is 1894, when a Regatta Week was held. This was organised by the Corinthian Sailing Club, which later became the Sidmouth Sailing Club.

The Sidmouth Folk Festival has, since the early 1950s changed life in the town for ten days or so in August each year.

Many harbour projects have been suggested but none have materialised but are still being discussed to the present day.

Was this part of the Regatta?

Another annual event, which started in the mid 1980s by the Sidmouth Round Table, is the Boxing Day Swim.

1985.

There have been many changes, as I have tried to research and record.

In Sidmouth as with all seaside towns, the weather has played a big part in the way that the town and sea front has changed over the years. Storms are still causing major expense, and cliff falls have always been happening, mostly on the eastern side.

Early writings say the river Sid used to reach the sea near where the Bedford Hotel is now situated today. Over the years the course of the river has moved eastwards until it came up against Salcombe cliffs. This was probably helped by man developing grazing land and building the town, and additionally the building of a harbour around 1300 would have drained some land.

The eastern side of what is now the High Street, Church Lane, Old Fore Street, was marshland.

William Day's map of 1789 shows the beach with very little development along the foreshore. Most of the town was set back from the beach and consisted of cottages, some very tightly packed together, small shops, and the local people would have consisted of fishermen, farmers, and a mixture of small traders.

In 1801 there were about 240 houses and 1250 inhabitants. 1861, 537 houses and 2572 inhabitants, and comprised 1,540 acres of land and 60 acres of water.

Where the Esplanade now stands there was only a natural ridge of shingle and rough grass. There were pathways between the few buildings and the sea. In 1805 a mud and flint bank was built up, and although this was an improvement the sea did come over into the town in really bad weather.

Up to 1836 there was still only a bank of earth and shingle with a rough track walkway on top with wooden posts on the seaside.

In about 1780 the eastern end, between what is now called Fore Street and Ham Lane was a dockyard for building ships. It faced the sea and three boats on stocks could be built simultaneously. These were pulled over the beach and launched. Some were taken to Exmouth for rigging.

The last reference I have found for one being launched was on the 28th September 1850. This may have been the last ship to be built here.

A document dated 3rd June 1322 concerning a dispute over the boundary of Sidmouth and Salcombe Regis. It writes that there was a Port at the mouth of the river Sid. So there must have been a small natural harbour, deep enough for fishing boats to dock and unload their catch. This could have been the start of the name 'Port Royal' because another document of 1347, states 'All ships lying in harbour to be seized for the King's use'.

This area silted up and became marshland. It then became 'The Marsh', and not so many years ago some of the old locals still called it by that name.

The main trades were fishing, farming, and boat building. The 1921 census showed 2747 inhabitants, with 6 Schools, 5 Pubs, 13 Boot and Shoe Makers, 6 Tailors, 5 Bakers, 3 Butchers.

Boat building must have also employed many men, with the boatyards. Another 'trade' was smuggling. Vernon Bartlett wrote about it and the Sidmouth Herald published some of his writings. He also wrote a paper headed 'Freetrading Days in 1885'.

'Fishing and free-trading (or smuggling, as we would call it now) were the two main industries in Sidmouth up to about 1840. Many well-known and respected people were into smuggling, and there were close connections with the church, but it was not considered a crime. Ladram, Windgates, Salcombe Mouth and Weston were much favoured landing places'. The people were good tempered and pulled together. Sidbury financed, and Branscombe landed the goods, whilst Sidmouth found the wagons and Salcombe the carriers.

Gradually as time passed the town attracted visitors, in the form of wealthy families renting rooms or houses for the summer, and so bringing new trade to Sidmouth.

In 1836 T. H. Mogridge wrote that: 'Sidmouth may be considered a dairy parish, pasturage is abundant, and, like most parts of Devon, is celebrated for clotted cream'.

Fishing was one of the main sources of income. Many fishermen had families to support and in the winter when life was hard, the weather and fish stocks controlled the money coming in.

In Risdon's 'Survey of Devon' it was recorded that in July 1809, over 15,000 mackerel were brought in by one haul. It goes on to say, 'that the produce of each haul is divided in the following manner; the owner of the seine and boat is entitled to one half of the fish caught, and also to an equal share of the remainder with the rest of the crew'. With all this fish and no refrigerators the fishermen would not have made much money from a single catch. However, it was not always like that. In February 1899 a meeting was held by The General Purposes Committee of The Council in the Manor Hall to consider what could be done for alleviating distress among the Sidmouth fishermen. One of the principle causes was the failure of the fishing season. It was suggested that the fishermen could be given some relief work, such as raising and levelling the Ham meadow. The work was to be supervised by the Surveyor and the men to be paid 4d. for each ten barrow loads of soil or rubble. The money was to be paid out of the rates, but Mr. Skinner thought they should be paid a fair wage, and a weekly wage of 15s. 0d. was agreed. All those members of the fishing industry requiring aid were employed at the Ham area for seven weeks work, and this cost about £177. The sick and aged were relieved with grants amounting to £16 3s. 9d. Later in the year, Mr. Berwick's estimate of £49.13s. 6d. was accepted for supplying and planting tress and shrubs on the Ham Meadow.

The 1900s was probably the time of the biggest catches of local fish from around the bay, mainly herring and mackerel. Other fish caught included, Sole, Red Mullet, John Dory, Turbot, Shellfish, Crabs, Lobsters, Shrimps and Prawns.

Vernon Bartlett's notes about the drifters and fishing boats stated there were twenty three drifters in 1909. Sometimes up to eighty different types of boat would put out to sea fishing, and laying nets. These would be marked with buoys and left for a few hours. On their return the nets were full.

Some of the names I have found for working with drifters in the 1900s are: Ash, Baron, Bartlett, Barnard, Bolt, Conant, Farrant, Hayman, Heffer, Hook, Horn, Pike, Radford, Roycroft, Richards, Salter, Smallbridge, Mortimore, Ware and Woolley.

Most of the drifters had names, the names I have found; Harvester, Samantha Jane, Loria, Stormy Petrol, Pride of the Ocean and Albina.

Vernon Bartlett also wrote: 'However, the local fishing industry was already failing (1909) and the sudden disappearance of herring, which was the main source of income in winter brought about the 'big exodus'. The fishermen, and my father among them, whose fore fathers had been fishermen here since time out of mind, all with families to support, were forced to find jobs ashore, locally and as far afield as Australia, Canada and south Africa.'

The Ware Family and "Forget Me Not".

A good catch, about 1905.

Bob and Harry Woolley.

10

This was also about the time that Mr. Stephen Reynolds came to Sidmouth (about 1903). He must have walked to Sidmouth, and not known any one, as one morning Bob Woolley found one of his boats turned upside down on the beach. He upturned it and found Stephen Reynolds asleep underneath it. He took him to the Woolley's home in Bedford Square, and gave him a good meal. They must have got on well together as Stephen went on to stay with the family for many years.

Reynolds wrote about a fishing trip, 'Bob and Tom Woolley one Saturday night about 5 o'clock, shot seven nets, 240 fathom altogether, 6 fathom deep. 27 drifters were out that night. By 7 o'clock the nets were sagging in the water. On hauling in the catch their boats were often in danger of being over loaded with catches of 22,000 herring. Back to the beach they had to have two boats to unload part of their catch before they ran their drifters onto the beach.'

Stephen worked hard with, and for, the local fishermen. Later running pleasure trips around the bay in his boat the 'Puffin'.

The Puffin was built in Dartmouth in 1910, to an original design by Stephen Reynolds and Tom Woolley, for working from the shingle beach, I believe this was the first motor powered boat in Sidmouth. Her engine was powerful enough to tow drifters, with a speed up to 8 miles an hour. Many a fishing crew were glad to be towed to or from the fishing grounds. Gradually most of the drifters had motor engines of their own. The Puffin worked off Sidmouth beach for many years. On 7th September 1936, after twenty-six years in Sidmouth she was past repair and was taken away by lorry to Plymouth.

Stephen Reynolds continued to live with the Woolleys in Bedford Square until 1916 when he moved to Hope Cottage with Bob Woolley and this family. The move was probably made because of storms and the flooding they caused to their home in Bedford Square. In October where storms once again sent waves over the Esplanade causing one of the biggest floods, smashing boats and flooding all the lower parts of the town. Ground floors of houses from Western Town and Eastern Town were badly damaged, with Bedford Square one of the worst effected part of the area.

Stephen did his best to stop the wholesale removal of shingle and sand from the beach. So much had been taken by the Manor and the Local Board that the beach was down to a very low level. It was not being replaced by the normal tides. Stephen in April 1907, went to the Board of Trade, and a year later they made an order banning the removal of shingle and sand from the foreshore.

By 1914, Stephen Reynolds was the Fisheries Adviser to the Development Commissioners. In August he was appointed by the Board of Fisheries to visit the fishing ports and stations of the west country and Dorsetshire, to ascertain, as quickly as possible, how far the fisheries are likely to be affected by the war, how far and by what means they best be kept going, what amount of distress and unemployment is to be anticipated among fishermen.

He wrote the book, 'Poor Man's House' describing life as a fisherman based on his stay in Sidmouth, In the book he called the town 'Seacombe'. Instead of Woolley he called them 'Widger'. He died in 1919, aged 38 of influenza and was buried in Sidmouth cemetery.

A faded inscription read "In memory of Stephen Reynolds, Writer and Fisherman, 1881-1919."

There were many Sidmouth fishing families. There are several christian names for most families. A listing for 1619 under 'Masters and Mariners' showed; Ashlye, Cawly, Fortune, Gold, Hayman, Pyke, Laddsen, Wheaton, Whytter, Windsor. Later family names; Bagwell, Bartlett, Bolt, Conant, Cordey, Farrant, French, Harris, Hook, Holland, Tapley, Woolleys. One other name I have is for Charlie Merrifield. He had a boat called 'Willing Maid'.

Fishermen and their gear occupied a considerable portion of the beach and prom, with rowing boats, drifters, gangplanks, capstans etc. There were nets hanging out to dry on the sea wall, and the railings of the Drill Hall were often seen covered in nets. It was all part of every day life in the 1800s early 1900s along the sea front.

Fishermen each had a recognised place on the beach, this was 'their' part of the beach, where they launched and kept their boats and gear. Some had hand capstans for hauling up their boats.

At the western end of the main beach were: Pursey's boat and gear, Woolley, bathing machines and boats, near Bedford steps, Ware, Merrifield and Barnard boats and gear. Opposite the Marine, Bartlett's bathing machines. Next along was Farrant, boat and gear. Towards York Hotel, Hayman, Salter and Smith. Fred Bartlett and Soloman brothers. Along the beach eastwards. Hook, Horn, Tapley, Smallbridge, Searle, Pike, Bagwell and Richards, and near the Ham, Harris family.

On the Esplanade at the Corinthian Sailing Club, in the sailing season were very large zinc-topped lockers where they kept masts, sails oars etc.

Towering over all this was the Beacon Light which was opposite the York Hotel.

In a book on Sidmouth published by Whittaker and Co. of London, it speaks about the Esplanade in 1855:

> 'Sauntering along this well-kept walk I was amused by the charming variety of names given to the different boats, Frances, Louisa, Britannia, Six Sisters, Hope Well, Wave, William Henry, Mary Ann, Timothy, Friends, Ann Maria, Providence, Jenny Lind, and Ocean Queen.
>
> There appears to be a deficiency of wooden benches at the west end of this parade, there being five at the east half, except you count as seats eight or ten large stones, which people are sometimes glad to use as such, for want of better'.

Fishermens gear on the Prom.

Drying the nets.

Also on the beach some fishermen had small tin huts for their gear. Gangplanks that were used for passengers to board boats for trips out to sea as well as unloading fishing boats, from the shingle beach. These were made mostly of timber, with one end mounted on a pair of large wheels. These were pushed down to the waters edge for boats to pull in alongside. The capstans straddled the edge of the prom, with protruding foreleg of each one a hindrance to walkers. These were of two varieties, the older all wood with a long cylindrical neck sticking up through the cross shoulders and slotted for the insertion of the roughly hewn capstan bars. The fishermen were the horsepower for turning the capstans. The later model had a wrought-iron cruciform head bolted to the top of the stem that took up the steel cable. This was hooked on to their boats to pull them up the beach. The crosshead comprised of four channels to take the turning bars. Another hazard to the careless walker were the net-carriers, four legged, with wooden slats nailed crosswise on two doubled handled poles for carrying the large black fishing nets up and down the beach. Also various dome shaped wicker-work lobster pots weighted with a brick. Occasionally all this conglomeration of fishermen's chattels was a cause for complaint by the fussier visitor. In those days fishing gear could be left about on the prom and beach. There were no senseless vandals to burn or throw them into the sea.

Stan Bagwell making and repairing lobster pots. 1960.

Port Royal Beach. 2001.

Sidmouth beach is no longer busy with fishing and trips around the bay, as there are not so many boats or the fishermen to use them. The drifters are now gone. Fishing trips are still done by a few men, but we do not see the nets and pots, or all the gear that used to go with the fishing trade along the beach.

The next chapters look into some of the history of 'the seaside' part of Sidmouth from the west bay, and the beach below Peak Hill, to the eastern side of the bay, and just over the river Sid and the Salcombe Cliffs.

I have put the information into chapters, a lot of items overlap, and may have more detail in other chapters. Many locations I have named, as we know them today.

JACOBS LADDER BEACH

Jacobs Ladder Beach about 1907.

To the west of the town is a bay we now know as Jacobs Ladder Beach. About 1780 Emanuel Baruh Lousada, bought a house and land called Pick's Tenement, containing 125 acres of Peak Hill, including Jacobs Ladder beach. In 1796 he enlarged the building and called it Peak House. The house was sold in 1869 to the Sidmouth Manor Trustees. (Sid Vale Association newsletter 57) This was later destroyed by fire and in 1904 was rebuilt by Sir Thomas Dewey, in a different style, looking much the same today.
At some time the ownership of the beach changed to The Local Board.

The bay was reached by walking a short way up Otterton Road, (Peak Hill Road), or around the foot of the cliffs along the beach at low tide.
At the top of the cliffs there were Lime Kilns (until about 1854), and donkeys took Babbacombe limestone up paths from the beach to the kilns.
Before the ladder was built, there were other footpaths down the cliffs, and the first reference which I have found for a footpath from Windgates to the beach is 1894. This was further west along the beach than the ladder is now. A report in the paper of 1905 said that the footpath at Windgates had been repaired and was now in good order.
The first wooden ladder was built in 1871, and went down onto the pebble beach. A new design was approved, and a new ladder was built in 1899. This was reported as a 'great improvement'.

The cost of painting the ladder in 1901 was £3 5s.

The normal high tides did not reach so far up the beach in the 1800s, but as the bottom of the ladder was built off the pebbles, storms did wash the foundations away.

In 1934, work started for an 11 foot wall and concrete platform beneath the ladder, to prevent the erosion and undermining. The platform was extended westwards in 1936.

Jacobs Ladder Ladder beach about 1900.

Jacobs from Chit Rocks.

Jacobs Ladder beach about 1910.

In October 1958, Coastal protection work was approved for a concrete walkway to be built below Connaught Gardens, from the Jacobs Ladder platform along the beach to Clifton Beach. But not as far as the Esplanade, so leaving a stretch of beach between. The work was started at Jacobs Ladder. A mono railway was built for transporting materials along from the ladder for the building work, which was extended as the work progressed eastwards. The walkway was about 10 feet high with a dwarf wall on the seaside, cost £44,000.

Construction of the walkway. July 1958.

July 1959.

The finished walkway.

In 1962 the Council investigated the building of a Chine. This was for a single roadway from the cliff field down to the platform near the bottom of the ladder. This was agreed. The work started in the winter of 1963-4. Hundreds of tons of cliff were bulldozed out and pushed down to the beach to be washed away by the sea. The road was laid with a dwarf wall each side. The work was completed in 1964.

Cutting out the cliff to make a roadway down to the platform.

Work in progress on the Chineway 1963.
Note precarious tractor!

The Chineway with new beach tents, 1964.

New wooden beach huts were built at the bottom of the Chine in 1967, for the summer seasons and taken away in the winter.

The next major work was the construction of a walkway to connect the end of the walkway at Jacobs Ladder, to the Esplanade.
Fundraising was started with Freddie Wedderburn as Group Chairman. Events were held to reach the target of £73,000. The walkway was to form a level pavement, suitable for wheelchairs and pushchairs, across the beach by the existing wall of the properties of the private houses and hotel along the beach, to the slope up to the Esplanade.

Clifton beach before the new beach and walkway. 1967.

This was completed in July 1999. The opening ceremony, with the unveiling of a plaque on the wall above the walkway, was combined with a fund day of events to help raise the last £3,000 needed to pay for the work.

The opening ceremony was staged by the Clifton Walkway Group and the Sidmouth Inshore rescue service to boost their separate fundraising activities.

The events included: the walkway being represented by a 175 meter ribbon on which donations of £1 coins were invited to be placed, along with other collecting boxes; a helium-filled balloon race; The Lyme Regis Majorettes; Face painting and different events along the seafront. Entertainment was also given by Celia Monck's 'Young Singers' who gave a delightful contribution to the opening ceremony.

One of the main attractions was the arrival of the rescue helicopter with the SIRS lifeboat, giving a demonstration of a rescue at sea, and launching and recovering the lifeboat on their new trailer.

Constructing the Clifton walkway. 1999.

Clifton Beach before the Walkway and improvements.

Clifton beach and the completed Walkway.

25

CLIFTON BEACH and DAME PARTINGTON

In the early 1800's there were two small cottages on Clifton beach. One of these cottages was occupied by Mr Bolt, Fisherman, and his family. He had a pig sty and kept a cow on a small sward of land, and visitors where supposed to have been able to buy meat and junket from him.

I have not been able to find the owner or name for the second cottage, but the story of this cottage is quite famous.

In the early 1800s 'Dame Partington' was supposed to have lived here. She was a widow with three large sons, who were all fishermen and were terrified of her. They never married, and they didn't dare to, any more than going into her spotless cottage with their sea-boots on. There was a kind of locker outside the back door, in which clean dry socks were always kept. The three sons could be seen balancing on one foot apiece, while they took off their wet socks and put on dry ones, with Dame Partington keeping a sharp eye on them from the kitchen window.

The part of the story that locals remember begins with the great storm of 1824. Tis said that Dame Partington, at the height of the storm, with the sea breaking up to her front door, put on a pair of her son's boots and got her mop and set to work sweeping back the sea. Nothing, not even the Atlantic Ocean, was going to come into her cottage without her leave. She tried to broom back the sea and threw back buckets of sea-water from inside her cottage. But the sea won and the cottages were destroyed. This scene has often been re-enacted on carnival floats.

Clifton Beach.

Dame Partington defies the Atlantic.

From, An imaginary biography by Helen Simpson, in The Listener, August 25th 1936.

This story may have been made up by a Rev. Sydney Smith, a visitor to Sidmouth.
An imaginary biography, called 'Recollections of Dame Partington', was written by Helen Simpson and published in 'The Listener', in August 1936 and broadcast on the wireless. There was a violent storm on November 23rd 1824, and the cottages on Clifton beach were swept away.

Bibliographic record. E. Cobham Brewer 1810-1897. Dictionary of Phrase and Fable. 1898.
A taunt against those who try to withstand progress.

> The Rev. Sydney Smith, speaking on the Lords rejection of the Reform Bill, October, 1831, compares them to Dame Partington with her mop, trying to push back the Atlantic. "She was excellent," he says, "at a slop or puddle, but should never have meddled with a tempest."

THE SEA FRONT

Glen Road, with the Fortfield wall on the right.
Photo. W. Bray.

I will start at the western end of the sea front, at the bottom of Peak Hill Road and the junction of Glen Road, and work my way across to the Ham at the eastern end at the Salcombe Cliffs.

In 1628 the Privy Council suggested Sidmouth should have a fort to protect the town. The chosen site was a field on the corner of The Esplanade and Glen Road.
The fort was duly built, and was later to be known as 'The Battery'.

In 1794 there was a rumour of a French invasion. So the town raised eighty local men to man the battery, (In the 1801 census the population of the town was about 1252 and by 1811 was 1683). The fort had four twelve-pounder guns and one six-pounder field gun. About 1815 the fort was abandoned: two of the guns were used to prop up the church belfry and two used as gate-posts at a builder's yard. The field became known as the Fort Field.

In August 1859, again the threat of a French invasion brought a call in for fifty volunteers to man the defences. They were named 'The Second Devon Artillery Volunteers'. Their enrolment took place in the Town Hall in the Market Place on Thursday September 29th 1859. On November 25th two twenty four pounder guns arrived in the Market Place. The Volunteers marched with the guns to the Fortfield, positioned them overlooking the sea and were given instructions on how to load and fire them. A lot of drilling and practice over the following months was to follow but the guns were only ever fired once; this was for the Queen's birthday, a twenty-one gun salute, with a delay between firing of one minute.

The two guns on Peak hill.

One of the new guns on the Cricket field.

A drawing showing the Belmont and the fort gateway.

The period as a Fort ended and the guns were moved to Peak Hill in 1870 to the field that is now above the Chine path to Jacobs Ladder beach. In 1872 The Second Devon Artillery Volunteers were disbanded.

The Fort entrance is now the main entrance to the Belmont Hotel. The iron gates have gone but some of the stonework is still there.

On December 11th 1883, a meeting was held to form a Rifle Volunteer Company, Sir John Kennaway presided, and Mr. W. Hine-Haycock opened a Subscription list.

In 1884 the third Volunteer Battalion Devonshire Regiment, B Company, was formed, consisting of: Captain J. A. Orchard, Lieutenants B. G. Pullin and L. W. Durant, and about 100 rank and file. Their firing range was at Bulverton.

In June 1891 the Volunteers assembled in the Market Place for a parade and inspection, Captain J. A. Orchard was in command. Headed by the band they marched to the Fort Field where skirmishing took place. The men paraded back through the town to the Market Place, and their Headquarters in the Town Hall.

By 1897 they had moved their HQ to the Drill Hall, with J. A. Orchard as Captain, and Lieutenants: G. Vallance, and F. J. Potbury.

In a book 'The Sidmouth Volunteers' by John Tindall.
He writes:

'In Sidmouth on August 3rd 1914 there were rumours of war. What immediate resources were at hand at Sidmouth to face the great and gathering menace? There were National Reserve men, all enrolled in 1812. The organising secretary was Major Hastings. Over one hundred Sidmouth men had been training for two years before the war under the War Office Regulations, administered the Territorial Force Association. For some months after the war had been declared men from this force were employed as coast watchers from the Sid to Ladram Bay. Boy Scouts were also employed with them. The officers were: Major Hastings, Captains Potbury, Moore and Vallance, with the able co-operation of Sergeant-Major Mackie. These National Reservists later became members of the Royal Defence Corps.

For about ten months the coast watch was carried on by the 7th Devon Territorial Cyclists under Captain Watts, and afterwards, under Captain Hunter. Later the cyclists were withdrawn and Naval Reserve men took over. Local control was in the hands of Commander Adams R.N. Sidmouth became the radiating centre for East Devon Volunteer recruiting, and for the formation of local corps. It also became the head-quarters of the 5th V.B. Devon Regiment. Mr. E. P. Green and Dr. Stokes did excellent recruiting work.'

Moving back to the Fortfield.

In 1823 a group of local gentlemen had a lease of the Fort Field, and this was selected as the site of the new cricket club. In 1827 an application was made to the County Magistrate to enclose the Fort Field to fill in and level over the beaten track across the ground. The wall was built parallel to the Esplanade, and railings were constructed. A marquee was erected for members and friends. Soon after this the first Cricket House was built.

T. H. Mogridge writes in his: A Descriptive Sketch of Sidmouth in 1836.

'Another species of healthy and manly amusement consists in the game of Cricket, for which the Fort Field is appropriated. The Club, consisting of many of the gentlemen of Sidmouth and its vicinity, meet every Tuesday at eleven o'clock, from May to the end of August; and during an interval of the game dine together in the cricket house, a comfortable and convenient building erected in the field by the members'. He continues to mention the 'promenades in the cricket house – polite references to pints of cider and ale!'

In a book with the unusual title, 'Sidmouth; as it is, as it will be, and as it might be'. Published by Whittaker and Co. London in 1855. Sold by Harvey's Library, in Sidmouth.

'About the late James Clark, of Sid Abbey, and the Old Sidmouth Cricket Club, which was revived last year, although the funds are not in a very flourishing condition. The Treasurer Mr. T. Aston Coffin, and the Secretary, E. Molyneux-Steel, the whole management of the club is entrusted. Assisted by Mr. Charles Floyd, the club may hold on for a few more years, not for the want of subscribers as the want of active players'.

In 1879 Mr. Hine-Haycock, was lessee of the cricket field, and Hon. Secretary for the Club. The Rev. H. G. Clements, President. On February 9th 1880, the A.G.M was held in the York Hotel. The Rev. H. G. Clements presided. And those present included:
T. Kennet-Were, J. P. & J. G. G. Radford, Captain Bartlett, J. G. King, Captain Jolliffe, W. Hine-Haycock. The Rev. R. T. Thornton was assistant Secretary. Mr H. Drew assistant Treasurer. The financial balance was over £100.
The cricket ground was sold to the Cricket Club in 1935. A new pavilion was built in 1938.

The Rev. Edmund Butcher, in his book 'Beauties of Sidmouth', writes that 'the lodging house 'Belmont' stands upon a level with the Fortfield'.

By 1813 Sir Joseph Scott, Bart. was renting the house and shrubbery comprising about one acre and in 1817 the house had been extended into a double fronted house with verandas and bow windows. Next in 1866, Mr. Thornton of Knowle held the lease of the Fortfield for fourteen years. This may have been all the Fortfield ground.

I have also found the names: Mr. & Mrs. Scott, and a Major Barnes, but I don't believe they were the owners. The next owners were Mr. William Hine-Haycock in 1869-84. They were followed by Mr. and Mrs. R. H. Hatton-Wood, and in 1920 it was bought by Mr. Fitzgerald and opened in 1921 as a luxury Hotel, The Belmont.

The last part of the Fort Field on the Esplanade side contained two small cottages: Fortfield Cottages, with gardens at the front. Later to be called Fort Cottage, occupied in 1856 by the Rev. H. Fellows, and in 1870 by a Mr. William Bennett. In 1930 the Fort Café, Mrs. M Lock, and by 1935 into the 1950s as Fort Hotel, R. P. Griffin, proprietor. It later became the Fort Hotel & Café.

It is now the Fort Café on the ground floor and the rest of the building as Flats.

Next we come to Bedford Lawns. This is where the Hot Cross Bun handout started.

The Sidmouth Observer, Wednesday 13th April 1898, reported that the bakers of Sidmouth intimated their intention of discontinuing the sale of Hot Cross Buns on Good Friday. As a result sufficient funds were obtained for the purchase of 2,000 buns from M. Wheaton of Newton Poppleford. The Sidmouth Town Crier announced on the Thursday that buns would be given out to all the children of the parish on the Bedford Lawns on Good Friday between 8 and 9 am. Messrs Millen, Skinner and Glidden were in charge of the hand out.

In about 1908 the buns were giving out on the Ham. In 1914-1916 the Drill Hall was used and about 3,000 buns and 1,000 oranges and Easter eggs were distributed each year. There were a few breaks in the war years, and again in the mid 1920s to 1930, but the custom continued. In 1932 the Market Place was the distribution place.

Today, the Bedford car park is used, or if the weather is wet, the Manor Pavilion or the St. John Ambulance headquarters.

The BBC recording for the radio with a boy after getting his buns, 1957.

Councillor E. Whitton, opening the custom of giving out the buns, 1982.

In 1902 the 'Pierrots' gave nightly concerts on Bedford Lawns in the summer. In 1909 concert parties were given on a stage set up on the beach opposite the cricket field.

In 1908 the ground was levelled off and a bowling green was laid. This was the beginning of the Bowls Club. The green was re-laid in February 1911. However, the 1914/18 war and the winter gales and seawater destroyed the green. In May 1922 the Council decided that Coburg Field would be used for bowls and tennis.

Colonel Balfour offered the Bedford Lawn ground for sale in September 1922 for £750, and gave the Council first refusal. They turned it down, but Mr. W. A. Dagworthy bought it. After planning permission for the site to be built on was refused, Mr. Dagworthy put up railings on the southern boundary and used it for a stopping place and parking for Char-a bancs, and motor cars. This was not very popular, because of the disorderliness of passengers and the unsightly amount of paper and other refuse left by them. In addition Mr. Dagworthy had erected a tent in the part which remained enclosed by the fence and this was used as a concert room by touring Variety Parties.

We will move away for a moment from the seafront. The name of 'Dagworthy' started to appear in other parts of the town: Henry in Church Street in 1897; Charles, Cab Proprietor, in Russell Street in 1902, and William, in 1910 at Denby Place.

This was the time when the 'Car' was no longer a novelty. Mr. Lake, in 1907, erected a covered building on part of his yard in Russell Street for cars. In April 1911, Mr. William Dagworthy submitted plans to build a garage opposite the Three Corner Plot, with an entrance from Bedford Square and Station Road. This became 'The Western Garage'. In 1912 he had started a motor char-a-banc for trips to places of interest in the neighbourhood.

In July 1936 he had permission to install Petrol Pumps at his garage. Cars could drive in between the building and the pumps, as no vehicle could be served petrol whilst standing on the highway.

By 1919 most of the roads in the town were being tar-sprayed. Another problem the car brought was the question of speed. The S.U.D.C. suggested, 10 mph, with no result. 1921 after more complaints, 8 mph was suggested. But not until 1923 was a speed limit of 10 mph. imposed. Notices went up at Winslade, Station, Cotmaton and All Saints Roads.

In September 1930 a special meeting of the Urban District Council was called to decide on urgent measures to cope with overcrowding of motor cars on the sea front.

Mr. William Dagworthy started a coach service to take visitors up to the top of Peak and Salcombe Hills. He converted two Austin Landulettes in 1928, into a charabanc with open sides; the seats were the full width of the charabanc, and it had low gears for the very steep roads up to the top of hills. It was always called 'The Toastrack', and ran in the summer months. They did about 11 trips a day between 10am and 6pm.

The fares were: Peak Hill 8 pence and 1 shilling return, Salcombe 9 pence and 1 shilling and 3 pence return. The booking kiosk was in the Bedford Lawn car park.

They ran until 1956, when they were bought by Greenslades, but they did not run again because of the new safety regulations. It had many drivers over the years: a few of the names which I have found include: Mr. Bill Bailey, Mr. Bagwell, George Hodges, Jack Kibby and Fred Sheppard.

Photo's H. Clapp.

The Toastrack at Dagworthy's Car Park.

The Toastrack.

Crossing over Station Road.

On the corner site, John Wallis, in 1813 opened a new building known as 'Wallis's Marine Library'. This was extended in 1820. An article in the Sidmouth Herald in 1997 by Max Hooper, stated that in the 1830 edition of Pigot and Co. 'National Commercial Directory', Mr. John Wallis was a bookseller and stationer on the beach.

The Bedford Hotel. Picture A. W. Ellis about 1910.

In the 1850 and 1857 directories I have found the first listings for 'Bedford House' a Lodging House, and the name Mr William Barratt. By 1866 it was known as Bedford Hotel and Billiard Rooms, Mr William Cawey. It was followed as the Bedford Family Hotel. 1873-79 William Marmaduke Mitchell and in 1879 a John Millen, Millen's Bedford Hotel. In the 1886 Devon directory a Mrs. Bailey is listed as a private resident. This may have been part of the hotel in 1919, Benjamin Goss is listed as Proprietor, and in 1923 Mrs. M. Goss. In 1925 K. John.

In 1935 an advertisement in the 'Flying Post' was for G. H. Stevens, former Royal Marine Library, as the Bedford Family Hotel. This has been The Bedford Hotel ever since.

Crossing over the small side road by the Bedford Hotel.
The houses facing the sea in 1809 were known as; Marine, Portland House and Marine Place. The name and dates which I have found for these properties are shown below:
Marine House: Rev. H. Gibbs 1852; Thomas Radford 1857; Isaac Clode 1889.
Portland House: The Rev. G. E. Deacon 1852; as lodging house occupied by Mr. F. Brooks 1866; Mr. S. Copson 1894, as apartments; Mrs. Coulson advertised as having three Sitting and seven Bedrooms, Bath (hot & cold), Good Sanitary arrangements; Mrs. Sarah Warren, 1878; Miss Warren 1910.
Marine Place. Built in 1820. Numbers 1, 2, 3 & 4, were a terrace of three-storey lodging houses or apartments. However, of the names listed as being here, I have been unable to find out the names of the owners. For instance in 1857 directory ten names are listed.
The only likely owner is a Miss Mary A. Slocombe who is listed as a Lodging Housekeeper in 1856 at no. 4, and in 1857 for numbers. 3 & 4.

No. 1: Miss Ann Cooke 1857; E. Horn 1866.
No. 2: Mary Ann Sheppard 1850s. Mrs. Ellen; 1866. Edward Horn 1873 and in numbers 1 & 2 in 1878.
No. 3: Marsh Thomas MD; William Wheaton in 1850; Mrs. Myra Cross 1878; Alice Cross 1910.
No. 4: Mr. Sellek 1906; Burgoyne in 1919.

Marine Place.

In the late 1920's alterations were made to all four houses to make them into a Hotel. On July 16th 1930 the property opened as the Hotel Riviera, and the first name which I have found for the owner or proprietor is Mr. G. J. and Mrs. E. Ractliff.

Crossing over Chapel Street, the first building we come to was a Warehouse in 1851, occupied by Mr. Henry Mitchell, who ran a Carriage service to Exeter. Also for this corner in Chapel Street there was a garage, in the 1946 directory; Burgoyne's Marine Garage & Grey Car Booking Office, and Western Counties Swiss Touring Co.
The next property is The Marine Hotel, although the names listed here may not be the owners:
Mr. Thomas Radford as the Marine family Hotel in 1857; Mrs. E. Radford 1866; John Broom 1873-78; G. Ellis 1889. Mr James Burgoyne 1897 as a Pub.
The Burgoyne family ran the business as the Marine Hotel into the early 1970s. I believe it was rebuilt about 1900 as a single storey building with a flat roof. It was completely burnt down in the early hours of Monday December 6th 1920, but was soon rebuilt.

Next door is a small building. In 1991 the Charity CLIC bought the building for holidays for families of children suffering from cancer. They closed in February 2004, and the property is now private flats.

Next, walking eastwards: in 1891 these were Regency lodging houses with small front gardens and were known as Portland Terrace or Esplanade Terrace.
These were demolished and new houses built. The new buildings were realigned to follow the road and the gardens were dispensed with.
The first building we come to appears to have been two houses. The first one Hampton House: a Ladies Club, a popular social club in 1891. The second one became Oakleigh. In 1895 part of the building became The Sidmouth Brine Baths.
By 1935 Mrs. Hilda Mortimer had bought Oakleigh and it became The Kingswood.
Now both houses are The Kingswood Hotel.

The other buildings to Prospect Place were four Lodging Houses.
3 & 4: Charles Spencer 1878. The next listing is for Furnished Apartments with Mr. Percy Baron in 1910. This is the first reference as 'Devoran', and by 1938, Mr. James Burgoyne, 'Devoran Private Hotel'.

1 & 2, Apartments.
The first name and date as Elizabeth House, Private Apartment or En Pension, when it was redecorated and enlarged in 1932. In 1939 'Elizabeth House Hotel' with Mrs. E. F. Brokenshaw, Proprietress.

The last site before Prospect Place was the site of, according to Peter Orlando Hutchinson: 'St. Peters Chapel dating from 1322. The pathway here was called, 'Go Church' later to be called 'Beach Street'. 'It is said to have been a Chapel of Ease, while Otterton was the Mother Church. The thickness of its stone walls, the firmness of its cement by which the stones were laid, and its Chapel-looking door-way arched with some certainty favoured this idea'.
It became a private dwelling. It was later used as a school and for a time as an Inn, known by the sign of an Anchor. The Feoffees of the poor held meetings there until the floor became too rotted and the building was pulled down in 1805.

Crossing over the side road (which leads to the back of the buildings):
In 1806 Marlborough Place was built, first as Lodging houses numbers 1 & 2.
I have not been able to find who the owner of this property was. Once again several names are listed, and they cannot all be owners. In 1878 it was listed as a Lodging House, and as Apartments by 1897.
It was later as one house called 'The Duke of Marlborough', and the next reference is for The Marlborough Hotel. In January 2004 it had new owners and new name: 'DUKES'.

The Marlborough Hotel.

The next site, situated on the corner of Prospect place and The Esplanade, has had quite a history.

Number 1 Prospect place was a Bath House with hot and cold showers. In 1805 the Sea Water Baths were opened, and after being patronised by H.R.H. the late Duke of Kent they were later named The Royal Baths. I do not have a date for when they closed. They then became Lodging houses, and the next names which I have for here are: Mrs. Roberts in 1836; William Bennington 1857 as Berlin Wool and fancy repositories. By 1890, they were listed as Apartments.

Number 3 Prospect Place is on the corner with the Esplanade. This was later (1923) to become the Mocha Café.
In 1780 the building on this site was known as 'The Shed'. This was a wooden shelter building with thatched roof and with benches on the ground floor. It was open fronted looking out to sea. John Wallis rebuilt the building again with an open front with benches. It was ornamented with stone pillars which supported a large billiard room. and a Marine Library which was open to the public.

John Wallis moved again westwards to the corner site that is now the Bedford Hotel and built a new building. A large sign stated 'Walis's Original Circulating Library & Reading Room'. The Library was open to the public on June 20th 1809.

The Sidmouth Journal stated in 1809:

'A lounging place in a pleasant conspicuous situation, where articles of fancy as well as information and utility may be met with. It is under the most favourable patronage, among whom we have the honour to boast Lord Gwyder and Lady Willoughby, Lord and Lady Le Despenser, Emanuel Baruh Lousada Esq., and principle nobility of the town and neighbourhood'.

The Rev. Butcher wrote in 1810 and in 1820:

'This is a very neat pile of a building with battlements. At the western extremity next to the Fort Field is a round tower with a flag-staff, on which the union is hoisted to celebrate the anniversary of each principal victory during the late war, as well as upon royal birthdays and other particular occasions.

It has a veranda 42 feet in length, under one half of which was a retreat from the sun 15 feet deep, surrounded with seats.

A place in a conspicuous and pleasant situation, good view of the sea and opens directly on to the promenade, where all the beauty and fashion of the place are often collected. It is well supplied every day with London and provincial newspapers. Several of the most popular periodical publications are to be found upon the tables. A variety of elegant toys and trinkets, and some articles of greater utility occupy its shelves. Books of education, dissected maps and a circulating library'.

Wallis's Royal Marine Library, 1818.   *Westcountry Studies Library, Exeter.*

This became 'The Billiard, Reading, and Subscription Rooms'. By 1815 telescopes were also available for hire. It was noted that 'HMS Bellerophon' with Napoleon on board was seen off Sidmouth on its way to Torquay. All the telescopes were hired out for this event.

In a book on Sidmouth published by Whittaker and Co. of London in 1855, about the Esplanade, one reads:

'The cast-iron Drain Pipe, now emptying itself on the beach in front of the "Subscription Rooms" (that is in front of the building vulgarly blazoned forth as such in enormous black letters on a white board) might be continued one hundred and fifty feet further out to sea – in fact to below low water- I offer this hint to the Sidmouth Sanitary Improvement Committee, whoever they may be'.

Next door was Blossom House, one of the first houses to be built on the seafront in about 1795. This probably started as a Lodging House. The Rev. Butcher's writings for 1803: 'a billiard table had been installed on the ground floor and a reading room on the first floor, making it a popular place for visitors'. Sometime after the 1824 storm when, like many buildings were damaged, the front of the building was changed to the building we know today. The King family were here in 1850 -1897, and Mr. King changed the name to Beach House in 1884. Mr. E. G. Russell occupied the property in 1919. Miss Tilley Apartments in 1922, and in 1926 J. Skinner, Boarding House. In 1930s as Apartments, 1950s as a Hotel, still with the name, Skinner. It is now a private property.

On the corner of Fore Street is Temple House. In about 1805 this was a private residence, with a Miss Maguire. About 1872 it was leased to The London and South Western Bank. It stayed as a bank until 1970 when it became a shop.

Crossing over Fore Street, and walking eastwards to Ham Lane. The development of this area must have seen one the biggest changes to the whole of the sea front, as it gradually ended years of shipbuilding and the timber and coal yards. The site was all built on as Lodging houses, Hotels and Private resident's houses. These were all to become York Terrace. Plans were made for eight houses to be erected, and the first to be built, by June 1908, became numbers 1 & 2.

Gradually the first properties in York Terrace, Numbers 1 to 5, all became one Hotel, The Royal York & Faulkner Hotel.

One of the names I have is 'Yorkshire House' occupied by Mrs. Sawyer in 1826, and in 1866-1910 as Apartments. Unfortunately I have been unable to find the name of the owners or where the property was.

No. 1. The York Hotel. This was the first purpose built Hotel in the town, and opened in 1810. Mr. Richard Stone was the first proprietor. He rented the building from the Sidmouth Manor for the sum of £21 0s. 0d. p.a. for the Head Lease.

The Royal York Hotel. Advertisement in a hand book; The Summerland by the Sea, 1922.

In the great gale (as it became known) of November 24th 1824, Richard Stone suffered severe losses when his cellars were flooded causing destruction of all his valuable wines and spirits, not to mention the damage to the fabric of the Hotel. Richard died on August 18th 1831 aged 54. He was described as 'Master of the York Hotel'. His wife was Ann Taylor of Sidmouth and they had eight children.

In White's Directory 1850, Henry Joseph Hook Proprietor of the York Hotel.

The York Stables, also known as The Mews, were a little way up Fore Street, (Selley's Yard). Four-horse Coaches ran daily from here to Sidmouth Station and Honiton. Carriages and Horses were always for hire.

Royal York Hotel. 1920s.

Advertisement in the Sidmouth Directory and General Advertiser, 1870.

In 1878, John Chamberlain, as a wine and spirit merchant, omnibus proprietor, livery stable and job master. In 1887, William Rogers proprietor.

In 1894 it was advertised as a Family Hotel; 'The Oldest Established and Principal Hotel' in the town, Mrs. E. E. Barnard, Proprietress, and a National Telephone No. 2. By 1907 Miss M. Wright Proprietress, and a Telephone No. 43. In 1919 A. E. Mitchell, Proprietor. Next in 1926 Mrs. S. E. Pickard, and later Mr. and Mrs. Reggie Pickard until 1952.

An interesting note, in the Second World War this Hotel was not requisitioned by the services, and since the owner was also the Town Clerk to the Sidmouth Urban District Council, this caused more than a few local 'raised eyebrows'!

For a time it was owned by a group of local business men and in 1970 Peter and Rosemary Hook together with the family acquired the York Hotel and expanded to form the now, Royal York & Faulkner Hotel.

No. 2 Private house, only references found for this property, Miss Elizabeth Culverwell, 1883, and Richard Stone 1889. The first reference as 'Ulverstone House', is for apartments in 1910-26 with the name William Charles Hook. He was also a fishmonger with a shop in Fore Street..

No. 3: 1866-73 as a Lodging House and later as a small guest house.

The first date I have as, 'Faulkner Private Hotel', Mrs. A. M. Saunders, Proprietress, in 1926. In 1939 the property was bought by Freddie and Violet Hook.

No. 4: In Pigot & Co's Directory 1830, there is a reference; 'Royal library situated on York Terrace, are elegant assembly rooms', Miss Rose for about 1824-66.

Marsh's Assembly Rooms, and in 1851 it had been fitted out to accommodate lectures, parties, balls and auction sales. In 1883 as a lodging house.

I have been unable to find any more details until about 1946 when the Hook family bought No 4 from Misses Rolls, and became part of the Faulkner Hotel.

No. 5: 1820 Stocker & Longmore's New Baths. 1851 Brian Butter's Baths, to about 1866. It then became a lodging house, Mr Ebdon as a lodging house keeper, and also Mary Ebdon. 1883 John Patch, furnished apartments. No more details until 1922 Mrs. Hazlewood, High Class Apartments. Next in 1938 when it was advertised as Aldenham House, Private Hotel, F. J. Vanstone Proprietor by 1947 as Mr. and Mrs. Vanstone. 1949 as Aldenham House listed as four Flats.

About 1956 this property was bought from Mr. and Mrs. Sellick by the Hook family, and became part of the Faulkner Hotel.

No. 6: The first reference I have found for here is for 1947, when the occupier was Mr. and Mrs. F. Hoare. In 1949 it was listed as five flats. Mrs. Sellick in the early 1960s, and in the 1970s, Dr. Martin and the name Norman Cole, until the property was acquired by The Royal York Hotel in the mid 1990s. It became 'York House'. and is now the private accommodation for Peter and Rosemary's son Paul and daughter Sara, the third generation of the Hook family who are now running the Hotel.

One other interesting family note; Peter Hook was born in the original Faulkner Hotel (No.3 York Terrace) in 1940, and still lives with his wife Rosemary in accommodation at the enlarged Hotel (No. 5).

No. 7: 1857 - 1879. Lodging House. By 1930s I have the names Mrs. M. Trick and Mr. and Mrs. H. Charles. It became Wyndham House Private Hotel. In 1949 Mr. and Mrs T. Foyle as Wyndham Guest House, and by 1968 B. A. Foyle. Mr. Perryman changed it into Flats, and later became Wyndham House Self-Catering Holiday Apartments in about 1982. In 2004 Mr. Hook bought two first floor balcony flats which are now two suites for the York Hotel.

The ground floor is now 'Wyndham Court'.

No. 8: The first reference for here is Canterbury House, Miss Fayter, as furnished apartments in 1922. As Canterbury Private Hotel, Miss W. Nice Proprietress in 1930-1940.

The property was taken over by the Army in the Second World War, as well as No. 9 and 10, the next two properties. Next as three Flats in 1947. Mr. & Mrs. Tom Foyle in the late 1950s. For a time part of the house was taken in as part of No. 7 Wyndham. Later changed back to a private house. Now called Curzon House.

We will stop here for a moment, as from here to Ham Lane has changed more than any other part of the sea front, changing from industrial to hotels and private buildings.
This last part of the sea front was an important boat-building site, and later a coal yard.

In about 1780 about three boats could be built on stocks. Boats were built for the Newfoundland fishing trade. One of them was built by John Connant in 1788, and was named the 'Endeavour'. Small fishing craft and brigs were also built. They were then pulled over the beach and launched. Then they were taken to Exmouth, or to Topsham for rigging. One such boat was launched on the 28th September 1850. P. O. Hutchinson noted that in 1859 a small steamer was launched. 1861 a yacht 'The Star of Exe', and in 1862 'Rip Van Winkle' was built by Robert Leslie and Harry Conant. Some of these boats would sail down to Portugal where they took on empty barrels to store the fish, and then sailed up to Newfoundland for the fishing grounds.

The next site became a coal yard. This was used by Mr. Potbury who may have owned it. In 1865 the coal used to be brought in by sea in barges. These were run onto the beach at high tide and then unloaded by hand. The coal was then carried up to the yard, before the next high tide and barges re-floated off the beach. One of the vessels used to unload coal was the 'Samuel', which was wrecked in a storm off the western side of the bay in 1817. Most of the coal was for the gas works which was situated where the swimming pool is now.
My next reference for here is for Bradford and Sons in 1866. Then a Mr. Walter J. Miller bought the premises, and in 1878 Miller & Lilley & Madge was formed. They were coal, corn, slate, salt and lime merchants with timber yards. In 1883 it became known as Miller & Lilley, Corn & Timber Merchants.

In 1909 Mr. James Pepperell bought the western end of the boat yard and built three new houses there in 1911.
Mr. Pepperell lived in the first one which became No. 9 'Shenstone'.
The second house became a Manse for the Congregational Chapel, and the third house is now called Port Royal House.

No. 9: Shenstone. In 1932. Mr. & Mrs. Castleton, Shenstone Private Hotel. After the war, years, Mr. & Mrs. Stone lived here, and later Mr. and Mrs. Nash. It stayed as a Hotel until Mr. & Mrs. J. Govier bought the property in 1983, and it became a private house.

No.10 became an apartment house in the name of Mrs. Ebdon in 1922. It then became Huckers Guest House in the 1930s. I believe it then changed its name to The Seagull Hotel and was managed by Mrs. I. Hunt in the mid 1930s – 1940s. Number 10 now became the Strathmore Hotel when Mr. Bill Caldwell acquired it, but he was succeeded by Mr. & Mrs. Bess in 1949. The house is now called Port Royal House.

In 1923, Mr. Ernest Sutton bought the next part of the old boat yard and erected the first flats to be built on the Esplanade 'Carlton Mansions'. He was the husband of Anna, author of the book 'A Story of Sidmouth'.

The house is now Carlton Mansions as three flats, 1, 2 & 3.

The end site was cleared and a new building was built as garages. This became'Dean's Garage' when Mr. Alfred Dean, Motor Proprietor came in 1923.
The name 'DEANS GARAGE' was set in concrete over the main doors. In the right hand side of the garage for a few years was a Kiosk selling among other items, sweets and ice creams. Mr. & Mrs. Douglas Dean took over in the mid 1940s.
The Dean family were there until the building was demolished in 1988.

On the right side of the picture it shows where the houses used to end and the site of Dean's Garage.

Telephone No. 22.   Telegrams : "A. Dean, Sidmouth."

DEAN'S GARAGE,

Old Lifeboat House, SIDMOUTH.

Office : FORE STREET (next to York Hotel).

PETROL
AND
OILS.

REPAIRS
to all
kinds of
Cars.

HIGH-CLASS LANDAULETTE CARS FOR HIRE.

Motor Char-a-Banc Excursions Daily.

Private Parties arranged for.   Recommended by this Hotel.

The last building before Ham Lane was owned by the Burgoyne family. In the 1930s it became Burgoyne's Garage and Grey Cars (coaches) Booking Office. Over the next years various names have run business from here. In 1930 a Mr. F. W. Dowell ran a Carriers business from No 5 Temple Street, and by 1935 he was here as the Orange Motor Coach Service, going to Branscombe, Beer and Seaton.

In the mid 1940s, the Western Counties Swiss Touring Company Agents. By 1950 listed as 'Esplanade Garage'. Mr. P. Barns then took over, and in the 1960s, Ted Andrews was running the garage.

The end part of this building on the corner of Ham Lane was the R.N.L.B.I. the old Life Boat House with a side door in Ham Lane. After the lifeboat was withdrawn in 1912 the building was taken over and became part of the garage. The back of the building was used by the Council as a store, mostly consisting of deck chairs in the winter, and known as the Beach Store. I hear that some children were told this was where the beach was stored in the winter!

In 1964 the Folk Festival started to use it for one week in the year as an indoor song venue. It was thought not to be ideal for entertaining. It was done up as a sea-shore scene, with fishing nets, coloured tables, umbrellas, wooden casks and lobster pots etc.
It was used every year until 1986. The full story can be found in Derek Schofield's book 'The First Week in August'.

D. Dean, and Esplanade Garage.

All the garage and store were demolished to make way for a large block of flats in 1991, the new building called 'Trinity Court'. Only the stone pediment from the side doorway, with the initials R.N.L.B.I. remain, having been rebuilt into the side wall of the flats.

Trinity Court.

THE ESPLANADE

The 'Esplanade' originally consisted of a natural earth and pebble ridge. In 1805 the first attempt to create a promenade or walkway was when a rolled and flattened earth bank was constructed to form a broad walkway. This was nearly a third of a mile long, with the addition of a number or iron framed seats.

The Rev. Butcher in his book dated 1810, 'The Beauties of Sidmouth' wrote:
> 'The grand public Mall, is a delightful broad walk, upon the margin of the sea, railed and rolled in a very good style. It is nearly a third of a mile in length, and is furnished at the extremities, and in some other parts, with neatly painted, convenient double seats, from which either the land or the sea may be contemplated with every advantage'.

This though was not a success as the sea often kept washing over and flooding the town. The 'Great Storm' as it was called in 1924, turned attention to the need of protecting the town.

On the 14th September 1825, a special meeting of the Sidmouth Committee for managing the Public Walk was held, Henry Jenkins was in the Chair.
> 'Resolved, that the protection of the Beach and Walk from the incursions of the sea, is highly desirable for the accommodation of Visitors, and the prosperity of the town'.

The meeting decided that from Surveys and opinions of Engineers, it would be expedient to erect several groynes at intervals along the beach, together with an Embankment.

Subscriptions were opened to defray the expense. This was to be organised by: The bankers, Messrs Sanders and Co. and Messrs Flood, Lott and Co. The Committee for carrying the above plan into effect, Messrs Thomas and Henry Jenkins, William Stocker, Thomas Hodge, Francis Stevens, Michael Pile, Richard Stone and John March.

This seems to have been the first real attempt to protect the town from the sea, and also the first date I have for talk about the erection of groynes. The first date for their construction is 1875, when three open groynes were built. They performed well, breaking the force of the seas and building up the shingle and sand between each one of them.
At the time the Lord of the Manor was Captain Thomas Jenkins who lived in London and went bankrupt in 1835. The Manor was bought by Edwards Hughes, also of London. He had come to Sidmouth when funds were being raised to build an Esplanade.

On August 23rd 1834 at a public meeting, The Reverend William Jenkins presiding, it was resolved that the erection of a seawall was necessary.

The Lord of the Manor, E. H. B. Hughes was prepared to give £1,000 if the local inhabitants could raise a corresponding amount towards the building of a seawall, the plan and estimate to be approved by him and by a competent surveyor. Subscriptions of £1,756 10s were entered. A contract was made with Mr. James Clark Junior, for a wall 1,380 feet long at a cost of £2,150. An additional £45 was added for a flight of steps. The wall to be in a straight line, five feet thick at the base, four feet at the top. The coping was to be two feet six inches wide, with no stone less than four hundred pounds weight each. The Walkway, back filling was to be "the closest and most solid of gravel or earth". This was to be twenty feet wide and parallel with the wall. The whole of the wall, the counterparts of which were to be three feet square and not more than sixteen feet apart.

The work was to be completed by October 1835. A granite stone was set into the wall with the inscription.

"Erected at the expense of E. H. B. Hughes Esq.
Lord of the Manor and of Voluntary Contributors
in the year 1835.
George H. Julian Architect, James Clarke builder".

The foundation stone.

Access to the beach was by stone and concrete steps, known as York and Bedford steps. Opposite the Belmont Hotel at the west end of the Esplanade was a small stone and concrete breakwater built out for a few yards from the promenade. This became known as the 'Bump'. For a while there was a flight of stone steps opposite the Belmont Hotel, near the 'Bump'.

Later after the lower wall was built, for the summer months the Council put white wooden painted steps parallel with the wall, with a handrail on the right hand side, down onto the lower wall, giving access to the beach between the concrete steps. Taking them away to their yard in Manstone for the winter months.

One of the first dates I have found for chairs to be provided on the Esplanade is 1846, but very soon afterwards there were complaints that sailors and low people sat on them, when they were provided for subscribers and visitors. An inscription was then imprinted on then 'For Subscribers only'.

1900, The Council agreed to let the seats remain on the Esplanade throughout the winter.

June 1902, it was proposed that an extension of the Esplanade be made. This was to form a roadway, available for both foot and carriage traffic, from the existing Esplanade at Clifton Place to Jacobs Ladder, estimate £3,700. This did not happen; it was not until 1999 that part of this plan was carried out.

In the book on Sidmouth, published by Whittaker of London in 1855, reads:
'The sixty odd gas lamps might be more diverse and eccentric in their mountings, for example, some are set on neat iron posts-as on the Esplanade, others on white, green, or dark blue wooden posts, some on trees, one or two on top of railings, other on houses'.

The Esplanade about 1902.

In 1919 new lamps were put up along the Esplanade. They were painted red and each was fitted with one gas mantle. These were lit at dusk by a lamplighter. He carried a brass incandescent igniter on the end of a long pole. With a well-practised move he could turn on the gas tap and light the mantle.

The only name I have found for one of the gas lighters is Mr. Purchase, who according to Harry Daniell, 'could light the lamps without getting off his bicycle'.

The lights on the Esplanade were not lit during the 1914-18 war, and fell into disrepair. In September 1919 it was reported in the Sidmouth Observer, that the lights still had not been repaired, but by November it reported 'The lighting of the lamps has given much satisfaction'. In 1923 the Council stated that all public lamps were to be lit during the winter, and all lamp standards were to be painted green. In March 1927, a Councillor, advocated the replacement of all the Gas Lamps on the Esplanade to be replaced by electricity.

In the early 1900s large square shelters were built, open on all sides with wooden seats.

1903-1905: there were reports in the Sidmouth Herald that tons of shingle were being removed from the beach, and an inquiry was held between the Manor, the Council, builders and fishermen. The beach levels were dropping fast and not being replaced by the tides.

In the early 1900s large square shelters were built, open on all sides with seats.
1904: the Council said that boats would be able to be left on the Esplanade in rough weather.

November 1921: an 18 inch dwarf wall was built on the Esplanade along the roadside from the western end for a distance of 85 feet eastwards towards the Bedford Steps. It proved to be a great success and was extended to the York Hotel in 1923. In 1938 extended another 500 feet eastwards towards the Ham.
In October, the first new covered portable timber shelter was built, and placed opposite the Bedford Hotel. By 1928, there were three shelters. These were moved back to the other side of the road in winter. Railings were first put up on the southern side the Esplanade at the Clifton end and were painted dark green. In May 1936 they were extended from the Belmont to the Bedford steps. In 1996 they were extended all the way to Port Royal, now painted a dull grey.

1928: a new lower wall was built, on the beach in front of the sea wall with a base of six feet, narrowing to four feet at the top, this was about eight feet lower then the Esplanade.

1937: new shelters were constructed under the cricket field, looking out over the road to the sea. They are; eight feet in depth, 175 feet long, with a concrete roof level with the cricket field above. They were completed a year later.

1967 the Sidmouth General purposes Committee decided to adapt part of the west end of the shelter, a partition and door put in at a cost of £60, making it into an Information Bureau. This closed when they moved into part of the swimming pool building.

There is at the other end of the shelter a First Aid Post, opening at different times of the year.

New lamp standards on esplanade..

1952: The next major change came when the Council decided to have all new lamp standards all the way along the Esplanade, all to be specially made. These were to be approximately 26 ft. high made of 'Iroko', a hard wood from the Gold Coast, with twin lanterns. This was the first time in the United Kingdom this had been tried, and attracted a great deal of interest in the timber trade.

The following text is from The Timber Journal:

'An interesting example of timber entering a new field is afforded by the acceptance by Sidmouth Urban District Council, of designs prepared by the Timber Development Association, for lamp standards in timber instead of concrete construction of which has started. (The design has been slightly modified by the Council)'.

The estimated cost was £2,875 18s. 6d. the Council asked the Minister for transport.

The lamps were illuminated for the first time on Wednesday evening May 7th 1952.

By the 2000s lanterns and the wooden standards were all in need of repair, the wood was rotting and past repairing. The Council decided they all needed replacing. New designs were approved, painted black with victory-style lanterns and ornate brackets. Work started in December 2004, and by February 2005 all had been installed.

The New Lamp Standard.

The Bump and Clifton Place.

In January 1963 after a lot of debate, The Council, taking advice from their Consulting Engineer, decided that with a repair bill of £2,000 it was better to demolish the 'Bump', at a cost of £1,900, down to the level of the platform, which would be extended. Not without objections from the locals! In 1964 it was demolished.

THE BEACH

In the 1880s pleasure and fishing boats could be hired from the local fishermen.
J. Farrant & Sons. D. Hook & Sons. W Radford and S. Ware & Sons. All doing boat trips
and charging 2 shillings for the first hour and after that 1 shilling per hour.

An extract from Rev. E Butcher's book, Beauties of Devon, 1836:

'Pleasure Boats. Attended by expert and careful seamen are always ready, the
principal are set by J. & R. Bartlett, Thomas Heiffer, John Taylor, Henry Conant,
R. Bolt, W. Radford, T. Selley & T. Sanders.'

A two hour sail.	5s 0d.
To Exmouth and home.	£1 1s 0d.
To Dawlish or Teignmouth.	£1 5s 0d.
To Seaton.	£1 1s 0d.
To Lyme.	£1 1s 0d.

SIDMOUTH BEACH

The following are skilful, trustworthy, and experienced
men, knowing the Coast well, and may be thoroughly
depended on in the management of their

Pleasure or Fishing Boats

H. BARTLETT	DANIEL HOOK & SON
HENRY BARTLETT. Junr.	JOHN HOOK & SONS
THE BROS. CONANT	SAMUEL WARE & SONS
J. FARRANT & SONS	

Terms of Hire :—

THE FIRST HOUR, 2/-; AFTER, 1/- PER HOUR

FOR TRIPS TO

LYME REGIS, BEER, SEATON, BUDLEIGH-SALTERTON, EXMOUTH
DAWLISH, TEIGNMOUTH, AND TORQUAY

☞ SPECIAL ARRANGEMENTS CAN BE MADE

The inspection and practice of the Sidmouth
Life Boat "RIMMINGTON" takes place quarterly,
and these men and others belong to the Crew.

Advertisement early 1870s.

Other companies started to call into Sidmouth. An advert in 1878 was for steamer trips to Weymouth. In June 1897 the Steamer 'Victoria' was advertising trips to Torquay.

From a guide book 1905-6:

> 'It is common practice for steamers from Lyme Regis and Dartmouth to pick up holiday-makers on the beach. The steamers would put their bows ashore, and a gangplank to the beach enabling even women to get aboard without getting their feet wet'.

The Duchess of Devonshire.

The most remembered steamer to visit Sidmouth was 'The 'Duchess of Devonshire'. A 221-ton paddle steamer, which was built by R. & H. Blackwall on the Thames, the engine by John Penn, of Greenwich. She went into service in 1891. She was 170 feet long by 20 feet wide, with a draught of 8 foot 1 inch, with two cylinder compound engines. Top speed, 12 knots.

As she approached the shore, she would drop her stern Kedge anchor to hold her square to the beach, paying out cable, as she nosed gently onto the shingle. The stern anchor was drawn taut to hold her onto the beach. The gangway was the Ellett and Matthews beach landing gear. This was a 50 foot long gangway hoisted out by a davit over the port bow, so it could be raised or lowered onto the beach. Once lowered a small door in the bow bulwarks was opened and passengers made their precarious way down the gangway, helped by members of the crew.

Boarding The Duchess of Devonshire.

The Kedge anchor was generally of Admiralty pattern, used for kedging a ship from place to place, that is, the anchor is carried out to a distance from the ship and dropped. The ship is then pulled up to it by means of windlass or winches. I have not been able to find which anchor was used on the 'Duchess'. Most likely it was a Mushroom anchor or Stockless anchor; these were used by light-vessels on coastal or sandy beaches.

The 'Duchess' was an immediate success, so in 1895 her owners ordered her consort from the same yard, and she became 'The Duke of Devonshire'.

In July 1896 the first visit of the 'Duke' was reported in the Sidmouth Herald and Directory:

'A large concourse of spectators lined The Esplanade to welcome this new addition 'The Duke of Devonshire', to our coasting steamers. More spectators assembled on the foreshore in anticipation of a 'Trip around the bay'.

By 5.30 pm, the vessel, gaily decorated with flags, steamed proudly up to the beach, and disembarked between 200 and 300 people, who were privileged to ramble about the town for half-an-hour. About 100 Sidmouthians were taken aboard, and enjoyed very pleasant trip seawards'.

The vessel's length was 195 feet with a beam of 20 feet 6 inches. The engines, 600 horse-power. At 15 foot longer than 'The Duchess' and broader in proportion, she could carry 70 more passengers with first and second class saloons on the upper deck.

In June 1897 the Duchess of Devonshire attended the Naval review at Spithead, held in honour of Queen Victoria's Jubilee. She was also charted in 1902 for the Coronation Navel Review. After service in the First World War as transport ship in the Bristol Channel, the 'Duke' went to the Dardanelles as a minesweeper. Both ships were returned to their owners in 1920.

In April 1934 The 'Duchess' was in Exmouth Docks for alterations. One of the masts was removed and the bridge was brought forward of the funnel widening the sterns upper deck. The saloons improved. Also she was to sail under colours, the main colour, Oxford blue with white funnels.

They continued to run trips etc, but with the motor coach trade making its influence felt, the demand for steamers fell. The 'Duke' was withdrawn from service and sold. The 'Duchess' was also sold, but under the new owners, The South West Steamship Company, she continued to call at Sidmouth.

On Monday August 27th 1934 the Duchess of Devonshire sailed from Torquay at 10.30am, with about 45 passengers on board. It was an unpleasant day, wind and rain hindering her passage. She arrived off Sidmouth at 12.40. The tide was on the make, but there was an easterly swell and an onshore wind. It was said that the local fishermen said, 'if she tries to beach, she'll never get off again'. Captain Carter decided to put the kedge anchor down and run her onto the beach and make her usual beach landing. The very heavy swell caused her to drag her anchor, a second anchor was laid out but also failed to hold. This allowed her to veer and was driven ashore, broadside on, hitting one of the iron and timber groynes. She was holed below the water line. But on the falling tide she was high and dry. It was hoped that on the rising tide she could be refloated by the use of her own anchors. The Exmouth Harbour tug arrived that evening and the Duchess was pulled stern first out to sea. However the volume of water entering the ship was beyond the capacity of her pumps, so with her Kedge anchor laid out to hold her bow she was left grounded and the tug returned to Exmouth. A more powerful tug the 'Dencade' from Brixham was sent for. The hole was patched with cement and timber, but during the early hours of the 28th, the strong wind whipped up a heavy sea and the 'Duchess' anchors dragged and she beached. The tug 'Dencade' arrived at 7 am, and managed to get a towline aboard to refloat the vessel. She was then prepared for towing the 36 miles to the Dartmouth floating dock. However the temporary patch did not hold and she was making water fast. On the ebb tide she settled on another groyne, which holed her below the main dining saloon. The tug 'Dencade' left for Brixham. Once again the sea moved her and she hit the stone jetty causing more damage.

The 'Duchess' was declared a total loss and the scrappers cut her up where she lay. Not all was removed. The shingle covered part of the Keel, and it was not until May 1993 after a storm the shingle levels dropped and the remaining pieces were taken away. But some of the locals said 'Better she be left where she died'.

Fishermen Bagwell and Smith with four visitors.

F. S. Smith, E. E. Smith. E. Gamlin, H. M. Gamlin.

Trip to Sidmouth? Beach House top right.

Local fishermen carried on running boat trips around the bay and to Ladram Bay, mainly in their drifters. I believe that Stan Bagwell was the last one to run trips. New rules and regulations made it very difficult to keep going.

Trips around the bay 1960.

John Ankins and family on a trip round the Bay.

Whoopee Floats another way to paddle around the bay.

The floats were for hire during the summer months.

SIDMOUTH BATHS

In June 1791, (from the Exeter flying post). Mr. Taylor, a Sidmouth Surgeon erected conveniences for warm sea bathing and cold shower baths. However, I have not been able to find where this was.

Butcher in The Beauties of Sidmouth, 1810, writes of:

'A warm Sea Bath, the accommodation of which has been greatly improved by the present proprietor, Mr. Higham, has for some years been established opposite The London Inn, in Fore Street. A shower-bath forms part of this establishment.'

Mr. Higham was listed as a 'Medical gentleman'.

He also wrote in 1817 that there was a Mr Hodges at the Medical Baths, but did not say where they were!.

At the corner of Prospect Place and the Esplanade.

Sea Water Baths were opened in 1805, and after being patronised by H.R.H. the late Duke of Kent, they were later named 'The Royal Baths'.

Around 1820, at No. 5 York Terrace, Stocker & Longmore's New Baths.

1850-63, Mr. Barnabas Butter's Baths provided hot and cold showers. He is also in the 1856 directory as in the Market place.

The Public Baths and Social Club, photo J. A. Bellinger 1902.

Marine Hotel, The Baths, Lodging Houses and Apartments to Prospect Place about 1908.

A property built approximately 1881, the Architect, Mr. R. C. Murray, was later to become The Kingswood Hotel. In 1892 it was called 'Oakleigh.' This was a social club, with a large dining room, billiard room, lounge and reading room, later known as 'The Club,' with the Secretary, Mr. Kenandy. Part of the house was to change when The Sidmouth Baths Company Ltd. was formed. Designed by R. W. Sampson, the Manor Architect, they carried out alterations, with new buildings on the left side and at the back of the building to make the new Baths. This combined with a Social Club which was later called The Sidmouth Club.

On the 4th July 1894, the work of erecting the baths was started. They were to be called 'Sidmouth Brine Baths', comprising Hot and Cold Immersion Baths with heated fresh Sea Water, Swimming or Plunge Bath, Mineral Water Aix Massage Bath and a plain reclining bath with a capacity of 200 gallons of water.

The immersion bath.

The Aix Massage room, with reclining bath and shower.
All with heated sea water

Drawings by R. K. Sampson.

The finished swimming bath.

The Sidmouth Observer in July stated 'Problems with the sewer and drains during excavations'. On September 12th issue 'New plans submitted to Local Board, no drains being shown! October plans passed.

On Saturday April 27th 1895, at 3.30pm, the opening ceremony was carried out by Lady Bartlett, sister of the Lord of the Manor, Captain Balfour. Present included, Captain Balfour, Mr. W. H. Hastings, Dr. Williams and Mr. G. Scott, who had formed the company by raising the £6,000 capital.

The Billiards room of the social club was used for the reception, and The String Band played in the Reading Room.

The entrance, one shilling and six pence, or taken with a sea water shower, two shillings.

The Baths were renowned for their quality of the brine treatments for various ailments. The British Medical Journal wrote about the Baths 'The only Baths in Britain where the Aix massage is done with fresh sea water.'

The sea water was pumped up through pipes under the beach and Esplanade, to a reservoir at the back of the baths. The inlet end of the pipe was marked by a 'Bath Pole'.

Until a few years ago, part of the pipe work could be seen when the beach was low.

At a meeting of the Baths Company Ltd. Dr. W. H. Peile was appointed Medical Superintendent of the Baths. In 1896 the baths were improved and became more elaborate.

1897, Manager of the Baths Company was Mr. George Elkins and Mr. W. H. Hastings. Secretary, of The Sidmouth Club in 1902 the Baths Directors were, Major J. E. H. Balfour, D.S.O. Mr. J. Field. Mr. Pidsley, and Mr. A. J. Slade.

In the First World War, 1914-18, the War Office and the British Red Cross Society took over the baths, with The Officer Treatment Centre. This was for the treatment of injured officers. Peak House was the billet for the wounded and shell shocked troops.

At the end of the war documents show that the baths were not in satisfactory working condition. By 1918 the Baths Directors restored and extended the Baths, and added new features and modern appliances.

In 1923 the baths were losing money, but it was decided to keep going for another year. After a long closure, for improvements and upgrading the Baths were reopened with a grand ceremony in June 1924, by Mrs. Balfour. This was followed by dinner at the Victoria Hotel.

With the formation of a new company, The East Devon Brine Baths Ltd., some of the Hotels paid an annual subscription to the Baths Company. Their visitors had discount admission charge to the Baths. In 1932 this payment came to an end.

In 1929 under the supervision of Mr. and Mrs. Seymour Wilson, the number of treatments for the year were, 3,350 and had fallen to 3,150 by the end of 1930.

They never were a financial success again, and in March 1933 at a general meeting, it was stated that £1500 was needed to maintain the Baths. So by the end of 1935 the Baths closed.

I also have reference for part of the building as apartments at the same time as the Baths, part of the building must have been divided up.

In 1902 Mr. Richard Soloman, Coxswain of the lifeboat lived in Oakleigh House. In 1910 Mr. Lewis Downe was in residence.

Mrs Harriett Critchley was in the Kingswood apartments, 1906. Potbury & Sons, Auctioneers & House furnishers were also listed as being on the Esplanade in 1906. They may have been here as they were here in 1938, using the billiard room for furniture sales and as a store or warehouse.

1935, Charles Mortimer, town crier, lived in the Kingswood and by 1939 in Oakleigh House.

In 1938 the property was bought by Mr. Dagworthy. He leased the building. The next name I have for here is, Mr. Antonio and Mrs. Elsie Faulkner.

When Mr. Dagworthy died in 1951, Mr. George Seward bought the property.

Part of the old baths were used as an Aquarium, opening on June 18th 1960. A special feature was an octopus. Entrance, Adult 1 shilling. Child 6 pence. It also became a booking office for Dagworthy's Coach Tours.

The property is all now known as The Kingswood Hotel. Under the ownership, of Colin and Joy Seward.

Sidmouth had to wait until 1989 for new Swimming Baths.

The East Devon District Council was under the Chairmanship of Mr. Tom Fraser consultation was undertaken as to the position and appearance of a building. It was decided that the site of the old gasworks near the Ham would be used, then being used as a car park. Work commenced in October 1990. The site had to be cleared of all the remaining foundations and workings of the gasworks, and tons of material had to be taken away for disposal.

The Swimming Pool was opened on December 2nd 1991, Councillor Bill Thorne, Chairman of the E.D.D.C. unveiled a commemorative plaque. Sir Peter and Lady Emery were present along with dignitaries and interested parties. Children from All Saints and Manstone Schools took the plunge for the 'First Swim'. Geraldine James and Robert Ashby of the Sidmouth Swimming Pool Society placed £20,000 from the society's funds at the Council's disposal for extras at the pool. The Rotary and Round Table provided the chair and hoist for disabled swimmers.

Digging out the remains of the gas works.

SEA BATHING

Bathing in Sidmouth like other seaside places has changed a great deal over the years. Many years ago bathers has to be well covered up and had to change in a bathing-machine. The bathing-machine had to be wheeled into the sea, and the bathers had to get down the steps into the water without being seen. Then times changed and the bathers could be seen walking on the beach from the bathing hut in their swimming costumes into the water. In 1810, eight bathing machines had been placed on the beach, a little west of the town.

Persons who are fond of swimming, or prefer bathing without a bathing machine, should go to the west beach, where there is a fine secluded bay.

An extract from Rev. E. Butcher's book, Beauties of Devon, 1836:
'Bathing machine kept by Marmaduke Taylor, and Thomas Heifer for Gentelmen. Terms of bathing one shilling for the first time and six pence each time after.
By Mrs. Barnet & Co. for Ladies, one shilling and six pence first time and one shilling each time after.
Sea Baths (Warm) fitted up in an extremely convenient and comfortable style have been established both by Mr. Hodge, and Messer Stocker and Longmore; embraced every mode of bathing'.

Principal persons in the town offered other interest to the visitors in 1810.
Horses may be hired from: B. Butter, Painter. William Grove, Grocer and Druggist. William Gale and Matthew Hall, Linen drapers. Sam Pike, Cabinet maker, J. Peter Baker, W. C. Cawsey, Painters. Saddlers, Dunsford and Hill. Henry Smith, quiet and manageable donkeys with proper saddles for invalids. The latter supplies Asses` milk'.

The Sidmouth Herald published a picture in 1973, from Mr. Harry May, dated in a 1906 album of his, showing nude bathers on Jacobs Ladder beach.

In 1850, nine bathing machines. 1854, Complaints from the ladies who enjoyed 'sea bathing' about the men's bathing machines being too near to them. A report in 1864 stated 'no bathing machines or bathing for gentlemen in front of the Esplanade, or east of Chit rocks. All machines facing the Esplanade are for the use of ladies and children'.

Local bathing machines.

1873, The Local Board was to enforce By-laws to ensure proper use of bathing machines and proper bathing.

The bathing machines were all run by fishermen and their wives.

1899-1900 bathing machines owned by; Carslake and Bartlett the east end of the beach, Woodley's to the west end.

By 1911 the machines were also owned by Mr. Marmaduke Taylor and Thomas Heffer, for gentlemen and by Mr. Barrett & Co. for the ladies. Bathing without a machine was allowed in the bay west of the town (Jacobs ladder beach).

By 1914 bathing machines for gentlemen as well as Ladies were on the main beach.

The use of machines came to an end when small square tents, mostly white, some with vertical coloured strips were put above high tide line by the sea wall for the summer months. These were mostly supplied and managed by the Council.

By 1930s the S.U.D.C. had Bathing Tents for hire for changing in, and they put notices up to say 'No changing on the beach'.

Bathing tents started to be used.

Bathing Tents on Cifton Beach.

Tents changed to square shape and some had coloured stripes.

The Sidmouth Swimming and Life saving Society reported in the Sidmouth Herald on April 4th 1914, that the society had purchased a portable bathing shelter, and the Lord of the Manor had kindly consented to it being temporarily erected on the shore. This had been a great boon to the members. A diving board was also constructed.

The Swimming Club 1922.

Boxing Day Swim 1985.

THE BEACON LIGHT

In March 1872 the Local Board once again discussed the placing of a beacon light on the Esplanade, after the 'Margaret' ran aground on the shingle near Salcombe Cliffs. Three years previously a boatload of men and women landed on the shingle in the dark, after the sinking of their ship. This had shown again the desirability of a light. The streetlights are not lit on certain nights or during the summer and even if they were lit they were turned off at 1.00 am. A light would be a great benefit to local fishermen and other passing ships. After much discussion, Mr. Thornton of Knowle, offered to give to the Local Board on behalf of the town the ornamental pedestal and lamp standing outside his estate entrance in Station Road. This was gratefully accepted by the Local Board.

The lamp was originally erected by the tradesmen of the town, on which the inscription read:

> 'This ornamental pedestal and lamp was erected and placed here in November 1851 by the Tradesmen of the town of Sidmouth, in compliment to Thomas L. Fish Esq., of Knowle Cottage for his kindness in allowing his cottage and garden to be shown to the public on Mondays, for the period of over thirty years; whereby the Town of Sidmouth and its inhabitants have so greatly benefited. This column they beg he will consider a small token of their gratitude to him'.

The first Beacon Lamp.

The lamp was moved to the Esplanade opposite Marine House (Riviera Hotel). Mr. Barbour, Chief Officer of the Coast Guard at Sidmouth agreed that the gas lamp would be lit and extinguished by the men on duty, on a payment of one guinea a year by the Local board. The first lighting was on Monday 18th November 1872. However it was soon evident the light was not as effective as it should be, and not seen at the distance required. In January 1873 a red 'bull's-eye' was placed in front of the lamp facing the sea and a silver reflector placed at the back with a triple gas burner being used instead of a single flame one. This could be seen off Budleigh Salterton, and at a distance of four miles at least seawards.

In November 1881 the Local Board reported that a second light called the 'Fishermen's lamp' had appeared on the Esplanade. The Beacon Lamp had been moved to a position opposite the York Hotel. The board decided to remove this and replace it at once. All this had happened through the Gas Company refusing to supply gas as part of the contract to the second lamp.

In December The Board asked the makers of the lamp to supply an oil-fuelled lamp costing Two pounds fifteen shillings.

By May 1882 it was decided, in view of Mr. Dunning's attitude on the gas supply, to consider lighting the town by electricity.

The various lamps must have suffered a lot from sea spray and corrosion from salt, as they seem to have been repaired or replaced many times.

In 1891 at a meeting of the Local Board, the Chairman stated a new lantern was ready and should be placed on the Beacon lamp without delay. In September 1902 it was reported that a new lamp had been fixed on the Esplanade and was entirely satisfactory giving a brilliant light.

May 1910, an application by Mr. Hastings, Manor Secretary, to light the Beacon from the Victoria Hotel's electricity supply. The cable was to be encased in earthenware pipes on concrete foundations. This was agreed. The cost was about £21. By July the work had been completed.

August 1910, it was reported to the Council that a letter from The Brethren of Trinity House, complained of the unsatisfactory condition of the Beacon Lamp. In October it was agreed it was to be renewed. By February 1911 the Council had decided that the Beacon Lamp was to be repaired by Messrs C. J. Shaw & Co.

In August 1921 a complaint was reported in the Sidmouth Herald, 'of the non-lighting of the Beacon lamp. With the coming of the darker nights the need to those at sea is most necessary'.

In the great storm of 1924 the life of the Beacon Lamp ended when it was 'Swallowed up' by the sea. In the 1930s, there was a Fire Basket on a pole on the beach to guide Fishermen. This was destroyed by a storm in 1935.

This was the end of there being a special light for fishermen on the Esplanade.

The Beacon Lamp.

HAM LANE TO HAM FIELD

The main part of the Esplanade used to end at the Lifeboat slipway next to 'Marsh Lane', and is now called Ham Lane.

On the eastern corner of Ham Lane in 1790 there was a Preventative station. Sometime before 1873, it was rebuilt as a Coastguard Station. This building was built out into the roadway. It was later improved with new angled windows to give better views to the east and west.
Mr. John Baker was chief officer of the Coastguard Station in 1878, and George Ridge in 1897. In later years it was not being used and was closed in 1906.

In 1886 Coastguard houses were built on Alma Hill, and later part of the site was Coastlands, the home for the chief coastguard.
In a property sale report dated June 1906, called the Salcombe Hill Estate this comprised of about 148 acres. There was only one bid of £5,000 and this did not reach the reserve asking price. This was then offered in separate lots. One lot was the block of cottages, stores and gardens known as Coastguard Cottages, which were at the back of the buildings on the other side of Ham Lane.
Another lot was the Coastguard Station which was on the sea front and this went to Mr. J. A. Orchard for £450.

The Eastern end showing the Coastguard and the Timber Yard by Alma Bridge.

The coastguard building was demolished, and a single storey building was built on the site. I have no more details until the Life Saving Club used it in the late 1960s, and later as the Sidmouth Inshore Rescue Headquarters.

The next property eastwards was East Cliff House. Mr. J. Dunning, Manager of the gas works lived here in 1878 and in 1897 Mr. G. H. Appleyard became the manager.

In 1900 the road was made up, but was not tarred. Improvements were made to the Ham area. A footpath was levelled and tarred paving was laid, with granite kerbing, from the Boathouse to the Drill Hall. In 1902, improvements were made to the Public Toilets, and also to the Hanger pathways from Alma Bridge up to the Flagstaff.

It later became 1 & 2 East Cliff. By 1931 it became The East Cliff Guest House.
In the war years, 1939 - 1945, the Army used the building, and in a few years after the war it was in a dilapidated state and demolished.

East Cliff House. Photo from The Sidmouth News.

The concrete wall and the paved part of the Esplanade used to end here.

Eastern end showing the Coastguard Building and East Cliff House.

Photo 1970

Photo 2005

In January 1911 there was a proposal by The Council to purchase the remaining part of Alma fields and The Hanger, about five acres in all.

A children's playground was proposed in 1913, with a sheltered walk on the eastern side of the river. This did not take place, probably due to the outbreak of the First World War in 1914.

In the late 1920s, plans were made for the improvement of the Eastern end of the Esplanade and Ham area. The road was to be extended to Alma Bridge, and a children's play area was to be built. The steep steps on the Alma path were also to be reconstructed.

In 1928 the flagstaff on Salcombe Cliff was going to be moved back from the cliff edge because of the footpath falling away onto the beach. It was decided not to move it but to take it away.

In 1929 many car drivers were having difficulty turning at the eastern end of the Esplanade. So a large turning circle was built to allow drivers who drive to the end of the Esplanade believing that it was a through road to turn around.

There was more trouble with cars in September 1930, when a special meeting of the Urban District Council was called to decide measures to cope with overcrowding of motorcars parked on the seafront. In a letter, a resident claimed that he had seen 51 cars parked by the dwarf wall, while only 24 parked in the Bedford lawn park. Lodging-house keepers complained bitterly because of the distraction and said 'Visitors are becoming disgusted with the present conditions. Sidmouth's quiet summer charm appears to have disappeared'.

At the end of the Esplanade is the Ham Field, which was once waste ground and a rubbish tip. It became a public open space and children's play area.

Mr. John George Radford, in a letter to the Chairman & Members of the Urban District Council in 1896, stated:

> 'I propose to present to the town the use of the public field known as the 'Ham' now belonging to me (except a small portion already given to the Volunteers) subject to such conditions and stipulations as may be desired to be arranged'. It is only due to the late Chairman of the Local Board, Mr. Trump, to add that it was he who first suggested the desirability of the town becoming possessed of the 'Ham' and I much regret that he is not alive to see his wishes carried out'.

This was accepted by the Council. Work began on improvements in 1897.

Work started in 1899 on the building of a wall by the side of the river. It was to be six feet high, and would initially be about twenty-two yards long. It would be extended when further money was available. Local builders were invited to deposit rubbish against it on the field side, and the ground was then levelled.

In 1900 a belt of trees was planted near the Gas Works, and were fenced off. A year later the remaining part of the field and the rubbish tip were levelled and grassed.

More improvements were made in 1902. The next few years saw the whole of the Ham area levelled and grassed and the wall was extended along by the river.

In July 1930 at the monthly Council meeting there were two petitions. The first was for the retention and the second was for the removal of the chutes and swings from the playing field. The petition again drew attention to the unnecessary noise and disturbance caused by the children. The Council decided to move all the swings and chutes to the southern end of the Ham field.

In 1936 a new protecting wall with railings was built up-stream of the Alma Bridge. This was on the western side of the river and formed a walkway along the side of the river.

The last buildings before the Ham Field is the Shelter and Toilets.

Alma Bridge.

Down the path is Bagwell's Fish Shop and Yard.

THE SIDMOUTH SAILING CLUB.

In brief, a little information about the site and the club.

The earliest reference which I have found for organised boating and sailing, is for the Royal Alexandra Amateur Boating Club, in 1870-71, but I do not have any more details.

In later years the sailing in the bay was organised by The Corinthian Club, which was formed on Saturday 28th July 1894. In 1936 the name changed to The Sidmouth Sailing Club. The club rented the old coastguard building from the Council.

In 1954 another club was started The Sea Angling Club, and the first meeting was held in The London Hotel.

In the late 1960s the Sailing club members joined with the anglers to build new club headquarters which became know as The Port Royal Club.

In 1967 consent was given for a new Sailing Clubhouse to be built next to the Drill Hall on the site of East Cliff House. It was built by B. M. Vanstone and opened in June 1970.

Eastern end of the sea front by East Cliff House..

New Headquarters of The Sailing and Sea Angling Club.
Photo, The Sidmouth News November 1973

Rock breakwater and sailing boats July 2006..

The caption on this picture only states
OFFICERS OF THE DAY.
Photo by A. P. Holden
Picture loaned by the Sidmouth Sailing Club.

The picture was probably taken on the roof of the Marine Hotel. This was often used for announcements during events taking place along the sea front.

Sidmouth Corinthian Sailing Club.
Starting for the Club Race July 7 1898.
The picture was won at the Sidmouth Regatta in 1898 by Mr. R.W. Skinner's 'Valkyrie'.
Picture Loaned by Sidmouth Sailing Club.

The paddle steamer on the right must have been The Duchess of Devonshire, She had two very tall masts with a flag on each mast. In the picture the flag looks as if it is on top of Salcombe Hill.

Photo H. Fish, 1970. Loaned by Sidmouth Sailing Club.

THE DRILL HALL

In 1895, Mr. George Radford donated a piece of land near the Ham for a new building to be built. This was to be called 'The Drill Hall'. Mr. & Mrs. R. Hatton-Wood of 'Belmont' advanced money for the building work, £1,650. The building was opened on Tuesday 15th October 1895.

There were two inscription tablets, one each side of the entrance.
The left inscription read:

> The site of the hall was presented to the Volunteers of Sidmouth by J Radford Esq. of this town. The foundation stone was laid by Miss Constance Radford, on April 4th 1895. The opening ceremony was performed by Mrs. Kennet-Ware on the 15th October 1895.

The right inscription read:

> Volunteer Drill Hall for 'B' Company 3rd V.B.D.R. Sir John H. Kenaway Colonel; J. Albert Orchard, Captain 'B' Company. George H. Vallance, Fred J. Potbury. Lieutenants 'B' company. James Jerman (Exeter) F.R.I.A.
> Honorary Architect. R. Tucker & Sons (Sidmouth) Contractors. Cost £1,300.

The Drill Hall.

The Volunteers headed by their Band paraded through the streets before the ceremony. There were three Officers, Quarter Master Sergeant, Sergeant Instructor, four Sergeants, two Buglers and seventy other ranks. In the evening a company of 172 dined in the new hall.

The main hall is sixty feet long by thirty-two feet wide, and eighteen feet high. In the basement there are roomy stores and dressing rooms. The upper portion of the hall contained a subscription reading room, which was open to visitors, (in the late 1890s).

In the gable, over the entrance doors there was a clock supplied by Mr. Passmore; a watch and clock maker with a shop in the High Street.

In October 1903 Mr. & Mrs. Hatton-Wood presented the deeds to the Rifle Volunteer Company, which had been formed in 1883, wiping out the remaining construction bill of £600. The 3rd Battalion Devon Volunteers, Sidmouth Regiment, 1892.

The only names which I have found are: Lieutenants Vallance and Pullen; Captain Orchard; Sergeant Instructor Doyle; Colour Sergeant Skinner; Corporal Taylor; Privates, Potbury and Burgoyne.

By 1910, it was B Co. 4th Territorial Battalion Devonshire Regiment.

Apart from Public Meetings the Drill Hall has been used for many things. For 1814 I have: 'Sidmouth Theatre Licence, to Samuel Fisher of Teignmouth for 60 days'.

In November 1895 the County Council granted a Theatrical license for the hall. The first reference which I have found for this site is: 'The Sidmouth Pantomime Co.' production of Aladdin, script by Mr. Vallance, music by Mr. Bellamy and scenery Mr. Sampson. These are all local names.

On the 25th June 1902 the hall was used for the distribution of food as part of the local celebrations of the Coronation of King Edward V11.

From about 1902, Mr. A. W. Ellis, Photographer with a shop in the High Street, gave lantern slide shows. He purchased a Bioscope Lantern. This immensely pleased the crowded audiences. Later he started to have the new 'moving pictures', three shows a week with a matinée on Thursday's. Seats were priced at 1 shilling, 9 pence, and 4 pence. Next came the Talking pictures. The sound track was not on the film, but on a separate record. The speed of the film had to be adjusted to the speed of the record. This proved to be impossible and never worked. This soon changed and the sound track was put on to the side of the film. Mr. Ellis also showed films in The Manor Hall. By 1913 he had converted a shop in Fore Street (now Knights), to make it into a new cinema, and this seated 350 people. On December 1st 1905, a miniature rifle club was started here at The Drill Hall.

In April 1910 the hall was used for roller-skating. It could accommodate up to fifty or sixty skaters. The admission was three pence, and the hire of skate's nine pence. It opened on Wednesdays, Thursdays and Saturdays, and there were three sessions daily.

1911: Territorial Force Battalion. 4th Devon Regiment HQ.

1912: Sunday Services were held in the hall at 8 pm. In April, the distribution of the Easter Hot Cross Buns was held here.

During the 1914 -1918 War it was the headquarters of The Sidmouth Volunteers. National Reserve men were enrolled in 1812. Sidmouth men had been training for two years before the war under the War Office Regulations, administered by the Territorial Force Association.

On December 5th 1914 a contingent of 250 of Kitchener's men arrived and were billeted in the Drill Hall and the Manor Hall.

During the First World War it was the HQ. of the Sidmouth and District Volunteers. They were nicknamed 'The Old Crocks', and wore a grey uniform with a red armlet. They armed themselves to guard our coast, railway bridges and reservoirs.

The Sidmouth names were listed by Harry Daniell, in the Sidmouth Herald of October 1982. These were all once familiar names in Sidmouth, from businessmen, tradesmen, craftsmen and the gentry: Vallance, the Brewer; Potbury, Furnisher; Hasting, Manor Estate; Purcell, Churchwarden; Selwyn, Baker; Tindall, retired Solicitor; Skinner, Builder; Sanders, Estate Agent; Farrant, Harness Maker; Michelmore and Mossop, Solicitors; Passmore, Jeweller; Lake, Plumber; Till, Carpenter; Tedbury, Dairyman; Fitzgerald, Hotelier;. Mortimore, Shoemaker; Sellek, Ironmonger and General Gwynne, retired Commander. With the old soldiers Sergeants, Mackie, Page and Stoneman. This list also included the Rev. C. K. Woolcombe. There were also young men waiting to be called up: Barron, Hall, Power, Rickwood, Churchill and Mills. All received training in marching, signalling and shooting. Harry Daniell also recollected that for training on the rugby field, they dug a trench complete with a parapet, fire-step, traverses and communication from the Hospital side across to the grandstand. This was not appreciated by the rugby players! In 1920, the Drill Hall was granted a new Theatrical License, and became 'The Esplanade Pavilion'. This was used for live theatrical shows.

For 1923 I have a reference for the name Ernie Barry, Manager of the 'Summer Pavilion'. The next reference is for a Mr. Thomas Masters, He had the lease of the building, and he was manager of some of the London Theatres up until the Second World War when he joined the Army. He came back to Sidmouth after the war and introduced week by week Touring Companies to the town. In the Second World War years, the Army used the Hall.

One of the touring companies after the war in the summer was a seaside concert party called 'The Pierrots' who gave performances in the Drill Hall, and on the western end of the Esplanade and the Bedford Lawn.

In the 1940s, it was the H.Q. for the Sea Cadets Corps, The Air Training Corps, and in 1952 The Army Cadet Corps. It has also been used as a youth club, and for badminton.

Ernie Barry, Manager of the Summer Pavilion. 1923.

In 1964, the Folk Festival started to use the building, for one week each year. The first year it was used for accommodation, for fourteen women dancers. In 1965 as a Folk Song Club and by 1966 as a Night Club, with different groups singing, folk dancing and Morris dancing.

In 1967 the Hall was used as a canteen for the hostellers. The hall was used during Folk Festival Week, for dances, music workshops and late night events until 1994.

The venue's music and dance licence was withdrawn, much to the disappointment of many festival goers. It was then used, for one or two years as the Festival Headquarters for marketing, and stewards etc.

More information about the Folk Festival is available in a book by Derek Schofield: 'The First Week in August'.

THE ALMA BRIDGE

By the 1840s there was increasing agitation to have a new way of crossing the river Sid near the mouth of the river to shorten the distance for walkers to and from Salcombe Regis.

The Sid Vale Association, in 1846, agreed to build a bridge near the mouth of the river Sid, but the Salcombe Regis Lord of the Manor's wife; Mrs. Cornish, refused to grant access. On Sunday May 6th 1855 a meeting was again held with the idea to build a bridge. A deputation had seen Mrs. Cornish, who had finally consented for a bridge and its position over the river Sid at the mouth of the river. Eventually, after much discussion, an iron bridge was agreed, but the money was not forthcoming. Instead a wooden structure was approved.

The bridge was to be 125 feet long, 2 feet wide, and 8 feet above the river. It was to have five supports, planks and a 3 foot high handrail. It was to be made out of the timber from the ship wreck 'The Launer', and would cost £26. 10s.

The first Alma bridge, 1855.

A committee member was nominated to look after the bridge, which was named 'Alma Bridge' after the battle of Alma in the Crimean War. The bridge was erected by July 1855. In 1877 it was severely damaged and was nearly washed away. The Committee had it repaired, the cost £34.

There was also a series of steps made up from the bridge to the Flagstaff, on Salcombe cliff.

The second bridge.

In October 1895 it was proposed to build a new bridge, and it was decided to write to the Bishop of Madagascar, who was abroad at the time, as his permission had to be obtained. He was the owner of the eastern bank of the river. Mr. Sampson was to prepare specifications and get tenders for a wooden bridge on brick piers to be built at the same place as the existing bridge. Tenders were accepted from Mr. Butters for the bridge and Messrs Skinner for the brickwork. The new Alma Bridge was opened in November 1900. The bridge is in effect as the present bridge. Now with the new bridge, at a Council meeting on Friday January 4th 1901 a better approach was required. It was decided a good pathway could be made at a gradient of one in nine up the 'Hanger' so Bath Chairs could be taken up to the Flagstaff where good views could be obtained.

The New Alma Bridge.

The present bridge.

Alma Bridge from the Ham about 1905.

In 1987 the bridge was in need of repairs, at a cost of about £1,500. The committee discussed the cost. The Countryside Commission had offered 50 per cent, Devon County Council 30 per cent. It was suggested that the Town and East Devon District councils should share the remainder. The repairs included replacement of the missing masonry balls on the brick pillars.

Alma Bridge and the Drill Hall top right.

THE GAS WORKS

The Drill Hall and the Gas Works.

The first gas works built in Sidmouth were in Gas House Lane in 1835. (Water Lane). With workers cottages. The manager for many years was Mr. Paul Hayman.

In 1863, the second gas works were built at the eastern end of the Esplanade, now the site of the swimming pool and part of the Ham car park. Part of the old works were demolished, and a new Gasometer erected in 1870.

In The Sidmouth Journal and Directory, Dated March 1873. An advertisement.
    'Sidmouth Gas Works, to be sold by auction on April 4th.
    Now in the occupation of Mr. Henry Ellis, comprising the Land, Retort House, Cottages, Buildings, and Premises. Two Gasholders. Several miles of Mains, and 80 Public Lamps'.

In 1873, Mr. John Dunning, of Middlesborough, bought a long triangular strip of land near the Ham. This was under a Provisional Order entitled 'The Sidmouth Gas Order, 1874'. The new gas works were completed in 1874.

Mr. Dunning also obtained a further Provisional order for the purpose of erecting piers and landing places. He spent time and money, trying to build a pier or jetty to unload the coal barges instead of running the barges onto the beach to be unloaded.

Rough seas always destroyed all the work Mr Dunning put into building a jetty. In 1877 a storm destroyed the crane and the foundations were washed away. By 1879 he had to give up the idea. The arrival of the railway to Sidmouth in July 1874, meant that coal would be brought in by train, and then delivered by lorries to the gas works.

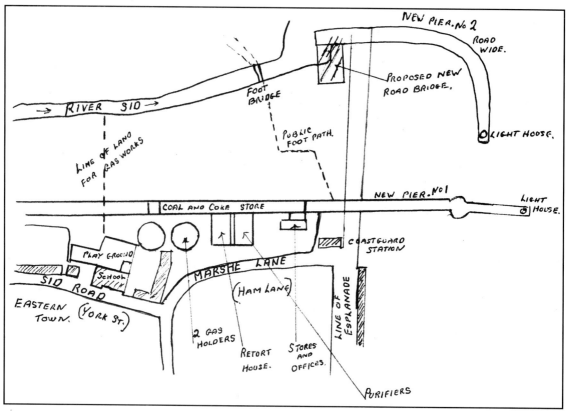

A sketch of Mr. John Dunning's proposed Gas Works in 1873, to be built on land near the mouth of the river Sid (The Ham Field).

By the late 1800s the Sidmouth Gas Company (Limited). Directors, Dr. T. H. S. Pullin, Mr. G. Pidsley, and Mr. Thomas Donglas, Managing Director. Secretary Mr. W. H. Hastings. By 1918 the Manager was Henry Burgess,

Lethaby's Sidmouth Journal & Directory, June 1872, contained an article under the heading 'The coal labour strike' and explained how coal was delivered to Sidmouth at this time.

'Coal vessels came into the bay and had to lay off some distance from the shore and transfer their cargo into large barge boats, which are rowed onto the beach at high tide. A. keel of coal was twenty one tons and to discharge a vessel of nine keels, or about one hundred and ninety tons, two boats were used with four men in each. They were paid 1 shilling and nine pence per keel per man. They struck to receive 2 shillings. As a vessel was laying off-shore waiting to be unloaded, the men would each receive 2 shillings and 3 pence'.

Post Card posted in 1910 shows the remains of a jetty.

The Sidmouth Urban Council bought out the Sidmouth Gas Company in 1913. In 1933 they built Gas show rooms in the High Street.

Gas consumption had risen from 18.000,000 cu. ft. a year to 70.000,000.

The Gas Works remained at the Ham until a new modern plant was built near The Railway Station, and this went into full production in 1941.

The plant was planned to produce 125.000,000 cu. ft. of gas annually. This in turn reached its capacity. Plans for an extension were suspended on instructions of the Ministry of Fuel and Power, and the closing of the works was in accord with the Gas Board's integration scheme.

With the integration of gas supplies to several towns in the region, the Sidmouth gas works were closed in 1956.

Site is now part of the Alexandria Industrial Estate.

Card posted in 1928, shows the jetty as just three block of stonework and the Esplanade completed.

When Dunning's pier was repaired some of the old blocks were not used and the local fishermen used them to make up a wall by the river on the sea side of Alma Bridge, Some of the blocks can just be seen at the bottom of the picture.

SEWERS AND DRAINS

In the mid 19th century, there was a growth in the town's population; 3,350 in 1867, rising to 4,401 in 1895. This led to concerns about the sewers and drains. Something had to be done to the existing systems and the lack of covered drainage. The surface drainage and the open drain at Alma Bridge required urgent attention, as at this time it was the deposit of nearly all the drains of the town.

A new local board was formed on May 20th 1863 and plans were made for a new drainage system. The aim was to affect an efficient discharge into the sea below the water line. A new tubular drain replaced the East Street drain. This was flat and too small, and this was laid by November 1864. By December 1866 it was announced that all the permissions had been obtained for a new sewer to be taken out to the sea between the Guard House and the river Sid.

The work commenced in March 1867 and was completed in September. In 1870 the construction began, on the Ham, of a liquidising plant. It was to have an underground sewage tank and a sea outfall pipe 42 yards out from the Esplanade. The system seems to have worked well both in good and bad weather. However, complaints were made about sewage on the beach, and float experiments showed that with a westward tide deposits of sewerage could come onto the beach. Therefore, more work was required, and it was proposed to construct under the Ham, an underground storage tank; 90 feet by 45 feet, that was capable of holding 1000,000 gallons. From this tank a new 2 foot cast iron outfall sewer would be laid under the river Sid out to sea in an easterly direction 400 yards long to below the low water line. The tanks penstock would be open, about on the half tide, and the tank would be discharged in an hour. The work was carried out in 1897.

In January 1959 the S.U..D.C. accepted a tender from Messrs M. MacLean Ltd. who were at the time carrying out sea defence work at the eastern end of the Esplanade. This was for a new sewer outfall costing £9,240.

Work started in March 1961 on the next big project for a new 1,500 foot sewerage outfall. Keir's were the main contractor.
Low loader lorries brought parts in to build a gantry which was to be floated out to sea for the divers to lay the pipes on the seabed.

Work on the Ham.1959.

The gantry being built.1961.

The gantry was bolted together like a giant Meccano set and lowered into the dredged out riverbed. Boatmen towed it out to sea and across to the seawall opposite the Belmont Hotel, where it was fully loaded with generators, air pumps, compressors and gas bottles. Additional buoyancy was added in preparation for towing it back to the river mouth and to position it between the two 250 ton concrete barges to start the pipe laying. However before the pipe laying could commence, an over night storm sank the gantry. It was top heavy and all the equipment was lost.

The remains of the gantry were towed back to the Ham. This time the gantry was built on two concrete barges. There was another storm overnight but the crane was winched to safety. The gantry remained at the mercy of the sea, capsized and disappeared.

The two barges also broke their moorings. One was washed up on western beach badly damaged, and had to be blown up. I do not know what happened to the other one. I don't it think was ever found.

There was one other disaster when an DUKW amphibious vehicle, towing the gantry, sank when it was snared by an anchor chain.

The concrete barge after the storm, 1961.

Following pictures taken by Mr. G. Reed.
Building the gantry ready for placing on the two barges.

Fitting the gantry onto the two concrete barges.

Ongoing work on the gantry.

Bad weather causing more problems.

107

A Derek was used to move the concrete pipes to the work site.

This could have been the end of the job, but Keir's manager was a Dutch man who had worked onland reclamation in Holland. He said they could build a railway out to sea. It had not been tried before. Workmen said 'will it work building a rail track so far out to sea?' The railway was build, 400 metres seaward.

The pipes were taken down to the railway. Upright piles were driven into the seabed.

The railway built out to sea. Photo by Mr. G. Read.

Work began on building the railway. The concrete pipes were taken from the works site on the Ham to the railway. The steam crane and pile driver would work from the railway. The upright piles were driven into the seabed, and the pipes were lowered for the drivers to fix them together along the seabed. Six divers laid the pipes, as tides and weather permitted. The wave action made working in shallow water difficult, and the pipes weighed up to 3 ton a piece. Altogether 72 pipes had to be laid. It was dangerous work, and cost the life of one local man, Mr. Roy Poole. A 150-ton jib of a derek crashed on top of him.

Keir's wanted to infill to the top of the piles to form a permanent jetty, but the council refused to have the plan changed.

The work was completed and was in use on Monday October 14th 1963.

This sewage system worked well for the next thirty years, but with the town's population growing, and environmental concerns with sewage outfalls into the sea it became necessary for a new system to be undertaken.

'START DATES FOR WORK ON A NEW SEWAGE PLANT'.

This was The Sidmouth Herald's Headline, of May 22nd 1999. South West Water to carry out the work for a treatment plant at Sidford. Two lines of pipes had to be laid underground through the Byes, under the ford at Millford Road, continuing down to The Ham. The Holding tanks, pumping station and all the associated works were to be located under The Ham playing field. The field at the bottom of Livonia Road, now called 'Margaret's Meadow', was the storage site for the pipes and building plant.

The Ham field became a construction site, and was surrounded by security fencing. Sewage was to be stored here and then pumped all the way back up to Sidford, where it would be processed. The bulk material was to be taken away by lorries. The water to be purified and returned by pipe to the Ham, and then out to sea.

Now, what must have been one of the deepest holes ever dug in Sidmouth got under way for the storage tank. This consisted of preformed concrete sections, which were made up into complete rings, and laid on the ground. The ground inside the rings was then dug out and the rings pushed down. Another layer was laid on top and all pressed down again, to a depth of thirty-five feet. Then a reinforced concrete base was added and a cover constructed over the top.

Construction of the main storage tank.

The construction site on the Ham.

A pumping station was built, with the aim of sending the untreated sewerage up to the treatment plant at Sidford. All the pipes and associated plant, storage tanks and buildings had to be below ground level, and the grass field reinstated.

The work was completed. The Ham field re-turfed, and there was an addition of two new raised flower beds. There was also a new paved area with seats, where boats used to be kept by the road.

HARBOURS

Harbours have been talked about for many years. In my researches I have found many harbour related items, and I have brought them together in this chapter.

Deeds of 1322 and writing of the time of Edward II and III suggested an open harbour. This may have been a natural mooring or a form of harbour.
The first talk of a new harbour seems to have been in the mid 1800s.

Mr. R. E. Wilson gave a talk to The Sid Vale Association members about Sidmouth ships. His report in the Sidmouth Herald stated that he had found that in 1302 Sidmouth in collaboration with Seaton provided one ship and crew to help their royal master, Edward I. He also wrote that in 1322, a writ was served on Sidmouth to provide three ships of not more than 50 tons and 75 men to help convey an army to Gascony. Further requisitions were made in 1333, and in 1338 to provide three ships.
In later years the demand was for larger ships, and the smaller ports were unable to provide these larger vessels. By the mid 1500s most of the small ports were silted up by sand and pebbles.

The 1300s were mentioned in Hutchinson's guide which was published about 1900.
He writes: a document showed that in 1347 all ships laying in harbour were to be seized for the king's use. He goes on to write that a number of writs of Edward II and III were written to the bailiffs or magistrates of the sea ports of any note in the kingdom. These are proof of an open harbour. He says the whole of Marsh Field or Ham probably formed an estuary where ships could lie in still water.'
A map drawn by P. O. Hutchinson in 1849 of Sidmouth shows at the mouth of the river Sid an 'Ancient Bay and Harbour'. This is depicted as being further over to the west than the river is now.

An estimate had been prepared for a harbour at the eastern end of the seafront by the river Sid in 1811. At a meeting in February 1812 the plans were presented, with an estimate for £15,252. 2s. 11d. This was to excavate a large basin in Marsh Field (The Ham) with an opening to the sea. But opposition from a party wanting to build on Chit Rocks at the western end lead to a stalemate and the project was shelved.

An advertisement in the Exeter Flying Post on September 10th 1812 stated:
'I Thomas Jenkins Esq. Lord of the Manor of Sidmouth, within the parish of Devon, do hereby give notice that I intend in the next session, to apply to Parliament for an Act to make a commodious harbour at or near Chit Rocks, within my said manor. Dated this 5th day of September 1812. Thomas Jenkins.'

The question of a harbour was again raised in 1825. An act of Parliament was obtained for constructing a harbour at the western end of the beach upon the Chit Rocks. The estimate for this work was £19,140. But once again this never materialised.

In 1836 once again tenders were put out for a harbour. This scheme was intended to enclose about ten acres on Chit Rocks. It was to be 1000 feet long and 500 feet wide. This was to be achieved by running out two stone piers into the sea, and forming an opening on the south east side. The stone for the construction was to come from Hook Ebb on the eastern side of the bay.

On Wednesday May 24th 1837, there was to be a grand procession starting at 11.00 a.m. from the Rev. W. Jenkins's Vicarage Court Yard, in Vicarage Road, to the Western Pier (Clifton Beach end of the Esplanade) for the laying of the foundation stones for the piers for The New Harbour. Two large blocks of squared stone had been procured and been floated out on rafts, and deposited on Chit Rocks, one to mark the place of the eastern pier and the other the western pier.

One of the foundation stones can still be seen at low tide when the sand level is low.

My daughter, Margaret on one of the foundations stones.

In June 1837 the Exeter Flying Post spoke of the event which had been timed to coincide with the the coming of age of Princess Victoria. This was 'one of the largest gatherings of people of all classes to the town we have witnessed.'

The event was started by a six-gun salute from the newly erected turreted wall of the Fort Field and the ringing of a bell, accompanied by the music the the South Devon and Honiton Bands parading through the streets, Lady Tompkin, representing her Imperial Highness the Grand Duchess Helena of Russia, who had stayed in Sidmouth for three months, shortly beforehand, performed the laying of the foundation stone of the eastern pier. The town's Freemason's in their full dress and regalia conducted the laying of the other stone of the western pier.

In the evening there was a grand public dinner to celebrate the occasion. The festivities were rounded off by a spectacular display of fireworks that lasted for nearly three hours, finishing just before midnight.

An advertisement for the Sidmouth Harbour Works, in 'The Globe' newspaper of August 8th 1838.

> 'Persons desirous of undertaking the execution of the several Works of this Harbour, may inspect the plans, sections, and specifications thereof at the Office of Alfred Lester, Clerk to the company.'

The proposed harbour looked as if it was going to be built. Ten acres were to be enclosed with a one hundred and sixty foot entrance.

In 1839 a railway tunnel was dug and track laid for about half a mile through the Salcombe cliffs from the Ham, over a trestle bridge over the river Sid, across the seafront to Chit Rocks. This was to transport rock and stone from Hook Ebb,
When the railway engine arrived it was too big to go into the tunnel, and so the tunnel was never used. Although the engine did run train rides across the sea front. Again the project was dropped.

But the townspeople undeterred, asked the great engineer, Brunel to help, and between 1856 and 1859, another set of plans was considered, but the harbour project was once again abandoned.

The tunnel entrance was blocked up many years later. Over the years the cliffs have been eroded away by rain and storms. In July 1955 about twenty yards of the tunnel near the entrance collapsed. More collapsed in 1969. By January 1995, more cliff falls, and about 10 yards of the tunnel were uncovered, opening up both ends of the tunnel. Over the following years most of the tunnel has been washed away by storms and cliff falls.

In 1863 another Act of Parliament was obtained. This was for a combined harbour and railway plan. The harbour was to be on the western side on the Chit Rocks. The estimate for the harbour was £30,000, and £90.000 for the railway. This was a great expense and the whole scheme was dropped.

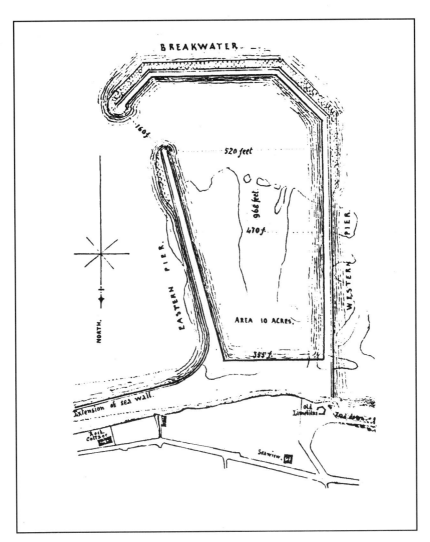

Design for a harbour on Chit Rocks. By W. Cubitt, 1836.

Sidmouth's intended Harbour. Published by J. Harvey.

In the following years the subject of a harbour recurred, and after the First World War the Board of Agriculture and Fisheries proposed the construction of a harbour as a peace memorial. The Councillors voted against it, and so another scheme was dropped.

As the years passed on, the harbour story, 'Should Sidmouth have a harbour'? is still being written about in the local paper.

In The Sidmouth Herald, October 7th 2005. Headlines read 'Nice idea – now we need £3m'. This was for a scheme to provide a safe haven for small boats at the eastern side near the river mouth. The project was to be called 'Port Royal Quay'.

STORMS AND MAINTAINENCE

Sidmouth, like all seaside towns, has always suffered from storm force winds, extra high tides and the pebble beach changing height with the power of the sea. A great deal of time and money has been spent on a form of barrier or sea defences to keep the sea out of the town, protect property, and the roadway near the beach. Sea levels are rising along our coasts and so this is an on-going problem.

The cliffs each side of our town are now being eroded more than they used to be by high tide levels, especially at the eastern end.

One of the first accounts which I have found was of a large fall of cliff at the eastern end of the beach, when in March 1897 a large part of Alma cliff and the 'Hanger' gave way blocking the river with boulders, trees and undergrowth. Local fishermen and workmen cleared the river.

The Jubilee Flagstaff used to stand upon the cliff above the Ham, next to the footpath up Salcombe Hill. In May 1909 a cliff fall took the edge of the cliff back to the Flagstaff, and disconnected one of the main stays. In January 1928 an extensive fall occurred at Pennington Point. Hundreds of tons of cliff fell onto the beach, and once again the cliff path had to be moved back.

After this it was decided not to move the Flagstaff back, but to remove it all together.

In June 1928 there was another large cliff fall and tons of the cliff fell down onto the beach, as far as the low water line.

There were more large falls in March 1933. The cliff footpath has been continually moved back, and in 1995 the cliff edge had moved so far back that the seating area at the top of the steps was closed off, and by 2000 the first length of the coast path was closed. Notices warning the danger of cliff falls were put up and the gate to the beach from Alma Bridge was locked, but walkers still ignore the signs and walk near the foot of the cliffs.

In 1936 Peak Hill Road collapsed onto the beach, and it was rebuilt back from the cliff edge. In February 1996 a bigger cliff fall meant that this time the road had to be moved further back through a field, and re-align a large section of the old road.

Peak Hill Road, 1936.

The 1996 collapse.

There was a violent storm on Tuesday November 23rd 1824. It was bad everywhere, but the south Devon coast was one of the worst areas, with Sidmouth badly hit.

After midnight with the tide rising, the wind increased in violence, and by 4 am the gale force storm was driving the sea up the beach. The tide was still on the make and getting higher all the time. There were two cottages on Clifton beach, and their windows and doors collapsed. All the inhabitants could do was to leave everything and get out, and shortly after the sea destroyed both cottages.

P. O. Hutchinson wrote about the storm:

'He said some of the sleepy inhabitants allowed the howling wind and rain to go unheeded, after all it was November, such weather was to be expected, but the rushing water in the streets, the breaking of doors and windows which let the tide into the houses, the falling chimneys and flying slates alerted them'.

This was not the only damage; the sea-front and the gardens of houses were covered in shingle. Doors and windows of Mr. Wallis's Library took the full force of the wind and waves, the water rushed right through, filling cellars and ground floors. He and his family escaped out of the back of the building into the narrow back alleys of Western Town. They got into a boat and were lucky to escape.

The sea also swept through Mr. Edmonson's Draper's shop (the site of Marine Bar) and the stock of silks and materials washed up into the town. Other houses were badly damaged and all the ground floors flooded with the seawater, sand and shingle. People had to be rescued from upper floor windows around the Market Square. Most of the homes and shops were flooded in New Street, Fore Street, Market Place and Prospect Place. Fishermen rowed their boats along Old Fore Street, New Street and Fore Street and rescued people, many of whom were in their nightclothes.

In Fore Street, Mrs. Sarah Street of The London Inn, lost stock and suffered damage to the property. Mr. John Pile, Ironmongers, as far up as the Commercial Inn, next door lost their stock which was under counter level. At Mr. Atkins, Chemists shop, the water pushed down the door and flooded the ground floor. Boxes of pills and medical packets floated out into the street.

In New Street, in Mr. Stone's Grocery Store. Mr. Stone went downstairs into the shop at about 4 am and found the floor flooded. He started to pass stock up the stairs to his wife to take up to an upper floor. But as his shop was one of the lowest in the street, and the water was still rising, he was soon up to his shoulders in water. Although he continued as fast as he could he had to give up.

In Church Street, Mr. Gale's Drapers was also flooded with loss of stock. In the Market Place, Mr. Longman, Druggist, also lost stock.

At Mr. Sparkes Hall's Drapers Shop, his son awoke about 3 am hearing an unusual amount of noise outside, and on calling his father was told that it was only a storm and to return to bed. His son could not sleep and made his way downstairs into the shop, to find he was over knee deep in water. His father did listen. The water rose over the counter and shelves and all the stock of silks, satins, woollens, and lace gloves became full of sand and seawater. After the storm a survey of stock showed over £1,000 was lost, a considerable sum in 1824.

Mr. Stone of the York Hotel lost large amounts of wine and liquor stored in the cellars.

This was also the night the Chit Rock was washed away. This was to be missed by the fishermen. This was used as a landmark for when they were out on fishing trips at night and in murky weather.

The rock had been important to local people. On one day every year there was a procession, at low tide, to the 'Chit Rock'. On the top, which was about 40 feet high, a man was crowned and enthroned, 'King of Chit'. The last King was Mr. Richard Bolt, a Sidmouth fisherman, he survived his kingdom for about 30 years. It was not until 1999 that the tradition of electing a King of Chit was to be revived. Mr. Bolt's daughter had married a Richard Patch, who lived in the cottage that is part, of what is now, The Swan Inn. A new monarch was chosen, The Swan Inn the place, and the name? Mr. Trevor Patch. He was crowned on Saturday June 19th 1999. His great, great grandfather was Mr. Bolt. The other local men to have this honour: 2000, John Govier; 2001 Stuart Hammond; 2002 Ewart Holland; 2003 Donald Slade; 2004 Jack Stokes; 2005 Garland Pickhard, 2006 Dave Salter.

In January 1873 the shingle was very low. This enabled an inspection to be made of the extent of under-mining of the seawall. This showed that the foundation was being washed away. Repair work began, but on January 18th the rough sea swept away much of the repair. On March 1st another violent storm hit the town. The waves were higher than usual, the roadway was deluged with water and pebbles and a large hole formed in the Esplanade opposite Fort Cottage. Part of the seawall was washed away in front of Clifton Place. The entire beach lost shingle and more of the seawall became exposed.

In May repairs were carried out and it was considered what had been done would be an effective barrier to protect the Esplanade. But in 1874 there were more storms and more damage. In 1875 several groynes had been installed which were successful in breaking the force of the sea, and consequently the shingle and sand began to build up between the groynes.

In 1876 there was further storm damage, and the town flooded, Milk etc. was delivered by boat as people were forced to move to upstairs rooms. Boats rowed around the Market Place, New Street and lower Fore Street.

Another Tremendous Storm was reported in the Sidmouth Observer on the 11th November 1916. 'The gale raged throughout Saturday and Sunday. Despite the fact that the tides were at the slackest, the town was flooded between 1am and 3 am. Great damage was done to property. Many boats were smashed. The Market Square was waist deep in seawater. Horses and ponies were taken out of their stables. The east end of the Esplanade was washed away by the force of the waves which left a jagged line of made-up ground only two yards away from the foundations of the Drill Hall. The gale abated in the middle of Sunday morning. A cargo ship the Steamer 'Grindon Hall', was driven ashore. All the crew were saved.

In October 1920 a series of storms battered the sea wall at the western end of the Esplanade. Large amounts of shingle were washed away and exposed the sea wall. Contractors endeavoured to protect the wall with shingle. Large crowds gathered at 9.30 pm. for the high tide, as huge sheets of water came over the wall and dispersed against the houses opposite. The wall survived mainly undamaged.

As the shingle had now gone, the first talks about railings were held. It was suggested having a small dwarf wall, eighteen inches high, by the roadway. This was discussed with the Contractors.

In November 1921 the dwarf wall was built from the western end, eighty feet eastwards to the Bedford steps. This worked well stopping most of the sea water flooding over the road. It was extended in November 1923 as far as The York Hotel.

In February 1922 the Esplanade was resurfaced and repairs to the face and foundations of the wall were done. Repairs to the centre groyne near Bedford steps were carried out. This worked well, building up the shingle, so in 1928 three more groynes were planned.

In 1932 the construction of a stone groyne, later to be known as 'The Bump' was built, as well as the existing timber and iron groynes. In 1935 the last timber and iron groyne was built at the western end of the beach, and in 1936 it was reported that shingle levels were very high.

1954 saw more work on the groynes. There had been a delay because of the problems of getting the right bolts to bolt the timber to the iron work.

The 'Bump' was demolished by the Council in 1964, as it was deemed too expensive to repair.

Over the next two years the groynes were not repaired and together with the lack of maintenance on the seawall, storm damage was again taking place. Therefore there were large holes on the Esplanade requiring repair. The foundations were not repaired.

The wood and iron groynes.

In November 1923 once again storms and high seas made large holes in the Esplanade. These were plugged, but again the winter storms broke down the wall and the town was badly flooded with more damage. Again in December holes were opened up on the Esplanade, and the town was flooded. This time the Gas and Electricity Works were also flooded.

In November and December 1924, gales and high seas destroyed a large part of the centre of the Esplanade and roadway from the Bedford Hotel to the York Hotel. Locals started moving furniture out of their cottages or up to the bedrooms. The gales and rough seas badly damaged many properties. The storm was from the southwest, at its worst around Christmas. By 5 am on Boxing day the sea was flooding the lower part of the town, Bedford Square, the Market area and Fore Street. High tide was about 6 am which made the flooding worse. Gas and electricity supplies were cut off. By New Years Eve the waves were scouring stones out of the Esplanade. On New Years Day, the Esplanade started to collapse, leaving a forty-five foot hole. The subsidence spread until part of the road was washed out. Traffic was banned, with the hole spreading over one hundred and twenty feet by thirty-five feet. Crowds gathered on the Esplanade to see the new Sidmouth sights. The storms had been mentioned on the 'Wireless' and even two Pathe Gazette news reel men came to film the damage.

The road was closed for months. The work to repair all the damage took a long time, as a great deal of the work could only be done when tides dropped low enough to work off the beach. The repairs took until early 1926 to complete, at a cost of £80,000.

Damage after the Great Gale.

Repairs to sea wall. 1926.

The work was completed, and preparations made for a formal opening of the Esplanade.

The grand opening ceremony was on Saturday March 20th 1926. A large archway was built across Station Road by the Bedford Hotel and Dagworthy's car park. The Right Honourable Wilfred Ashley M.P. Minster of Transport cut the tape. The ceremony was watched by hundreds of people, who then all walked through the archway to parade along the new Esplanade. After the opening ceremony, the dignitaries had dinner at the Royal York Hotel.

The splendid arch was built by a local builder, Mr. Ernie Barnard, of timber, lathes and canvas.

The Triumphal Arch built for the grand opening.

The Triumphal Arch.

Storms always bring sightseers to the sea front. The Sidmouth Herald reported on September 26th 1931, 'The highest tide for many years hit the Sidmouth shore, smashing a bathing machine and damaging several boats. A large crowd gathered on the cricket field to watch as the waves crashed against the wall.

In the winter we usually have storms with minor damage and flooding of roads. However, in January 1965, Sidmouth was hit by a severe south westerly gale and heavy rain increasing in force by about 2.30 am. The boats were hurriedly pulled back onto the Esplanade as seas swept over the road at Port Royal.

Jacobs Ladder beach suffered as a result of the combination of the height of the storm and the top of the high spring tide. The sea broke over the concrete platform and washed a large amount of cliff away. The wooden steps up to the café at the bottom of the clock tower were damaged and had to be dismantled later. The concrete steps from the platform to the beach, weighing several tons were washed thirty foot away from the wall.

In January 1974 the town just escaped serious flooding as flood defences held back the water. After three days of gale-force winds, heavy rain and extra high tides battered the Esplanade and town. Jacobs Ladder beach took a battering. The surface of the concrete platform was smashed up, and all the sand was scoured from the beach exposing the bare rocks. Work had started at the end of 1973 to strengthen and improve the sea defences and the concrete platform. This now had to stop for consultants to examine the damage and the cost of extra repairs.

The road across the seafront and promenade was covered in shingle, and some of the planks of wood used to block the gaps in the dwarf wall, which are put in the winter months, were washed away. The Sailing Club's boat launching ramp was broken up. A dinghy was washed over the dwarf wall towards Deans Garage. Most of the shingle was washed away along the full length of the main beach. The Clifton end was the worst affected. The river was dammed back by the shingle, and the river water rose to the top of the railings by the Ham field.

The Esplanade, despite the storms, did not suffer large amounts of damage for the next few years. The groynes helped to hold the shingle all along the beach for most of the time.

On Saturday December12th 1981 the sea whipped up by gale force winds, ripped up large pieces of tarmac, and a section at the edge of the seawall was broken away. Sections of railings were smashed. The road and pavements were covered in shingle, sea facing windows, such as one of Govier's shop windows and those of the Marine Bars were broken, causing the Bars to remain closed all evening.

In February 1991 all the face of the seawall was re-faced with new stonework, and the concrete capping to the edge of The Esplanade was renewed.

The Esplanade wall being refaced.

After more storms and damage to the sea wall in 1993, most of the pebble beach was washed away showing that the foundations, the seawall cladding and the red marl bedrock were being eroded. Major protection work was needed to protect The Esplanade and the town.

A defence scheme was drawn up, the final cost was a £6.5 million scheme to protect Sidmouth from the sea.

This involved a rock barrier to be placed at the base of the seawall, two offshore rock breakwaters built off the Chit rocks, and two rock groynes, and reinstatement of the beach.

1994: The scheme involved 125,000 tonnes of boulders, some up to ten tons each, and 165,000 tonnes of shingle. The contract was awarded to Dean and Dyball. Posford Duvivier, Consulting Engineers, and the work took from November 1994 until September 1995 to complete.

At first the rocks were brought in by sea on the Dutch side-loading barge, 'The Caelus'. Hydraulic rams tipped up one side of the deck for the rocks to be slid off into the sea at high tide. At low tide a huge crane type grabber, with its cabin specially raised above their caterpillar tracks, went out and fished out the rocks, one by one, bringing them back to the beach ready to be moved by dumper trucks and to be placed in position.

The barge tipping its deck to unload the boulders.

Crane grabs recovering the boulders.

As the work progressed the rocks were built into a causeway from the beach out to sea for the barges, which were towed in by a powerful tug boat, 'Goliath'. They could then be unloaded at any height of the tide and could be loaded straight onto the large dumper trucks. In April 1993 the boulders were brought in by road, two or up to five at a time on lorries. One Saturday afternoon a five ton boulder fell from a lorry as it came through Newton Poppleford. Demolished part of a garden wall and severely damaged a cottage. The lorry carried on towards Sidmouth with its unsecured load until Police stopped it on Four Elms Hill. The driver failed a breath test.

The new pebbles unloaded onto the beach.

The last part of the work was to bring in the 165,000 tons of pebbles, by road, and build up all the length of the beach, up to two meters below the top of the seawall.

The work was soon to be tested. In January 1996, a week of storms sent shingle from the beach across the seafront. About 60% of the beach had moved westwards or washed away. There were more storms in November, and once again there was shingle on the Esplanade with waves again breaking up against the sea wall by severe storm conditions from the east.

In February 1997 it was decided that a further rock groyne was needed at Bedford Steps. In November the Council's Environment and Planning Committee voted in favour of plans for the third groyne to be built, and the beach to be redistributed and the importation of more shingle. The cost of £350,000 would be paid for by the Ministry of Agriculture, Fisheries and Food.

In January 1998, the breakwater and sea defences were in the news again.
Sidmouth Herald, Saturday, January 10th, Headlines: 'Sidmouth's sea defences pass the acid test with flying colours'. Top marks for the sea defences: that was the verdict of the seafront hoteliers after waves driven by ferocious 80 mph gales lashed the seafront. Pebbles covered the promenade and the road was closed. Sky Television news transmitted news coverage.
This was the first real test of severe south-westerly gales since this major sea defence scheme was started in 1994.

The "New" Beach, and the two rock barriers.

THE LIFEBOATS

From about 1866 collections were made in Sidmouth on behalf of The Royal National Lifeboat Institution and a pillar collecting box was placed on the beach to receive donations for the R.N.L.I.

It had been indicated that Sidmouth would be the next place in Devon where a Lifeboat would be stationed. A number of boats had been presented to the Society in other seaside towns.

One donor, a Mrs. Rimington of London, expressed a wish that her boat be placed at Sidmouth, at the cost of £420. Captain Ross Ward RN. who was the Inspector of Lifeboats to the Institution, visited Sidmouth. He addressed a meeting of the Gentry and Trades people who had formed themselves into a committee to obtain annual subscriptions and donations for a Boathouse. Those present included: The Earl of Buckinghamshire, (who accepted the office of Patron of the Sidmouth's branch), the President, Mr. Thornton, Chairman Rev. H. G. J. Clements, Secretary Dr. Makenzie, and Capt. Joliffe, RN. W. M. Floyd, C. Slessor, Messrs. Bray, Dawe and Webber.

By August the Parent Society, the Lifeboat Institution, were anxious to place the boat on their stations before the equinoctial gales set in and would therefore send the boat down to Sidmouth, even before the boathouse was completed. Therefore September 25th 1896 was fixed for the reception and launch of the 'Rimington'.

The Lifeboat left the Woolfe's ship building boat yards for London's Waterloo Station, and was loaded onto a goods train for Honiton.

The boat arrived at Honiton station on Wednesday September 22nd, and a deputation from the committee met the train with eight horses, which were lent for the occasion by, Mr. C. Cornish (4), Mr. R. N. Thornton (2) and Mr. R. Gigg (2). The Lifeboat was hitched up to four pairs of horses, this was a set up the men and horses were not familiar with. Finally after a few adjustments and getting the horses settled, they began the long haul to Sidmouth. This was a six ton load.

The Honiton people turned out in great numbers to see the very unusual sight of a Lifeboat going through the town, and in the High Street it was brought to a standstill. Mr. J. C. Jerrard mounted the carriage and in a sort speech called for three cheers for Mrs. Rimington, which was cordially responded to. A long pull up Gittisham Hill followed. This was a major undertaking for such a large team.

At Sidbury the bells of St. Giles and St. Peter pealed in honour of the strange visitors to the village. People turned out to a child, to express sympathy with the lifeboat cause.

At Sidford, there was again a large crowd of spectators, and members of the crew came out to meet her. Then on to Sidmouth where she was placed in Mr. James Pepperell's field to await her launch.

The launch day was Saturday 25th 1869, and townspeople spend the morning decorating the town.

At 2.00 pm the procession left Mr. Pepperell's field in Vicarage Road. It was lead by the 2nd Devon Volunteer Artillery under the command of Col. Lousada, (of Peak House). The Brethren of the Ancient Order of Foresters of Sid Vale 4071 in full Regalia, and The Waterloo Friendly Society. Next, the Lifeboat on its transporting carriage drawn by the same eight horses as before, and supported on either side by the Coastguards under the Command of Mr. Barber RN. Then the Committee, the Inspector of Lifeboats, Contractors for the boathouse, leading Gentry and Trades-people. All the groups were represented in large numbers. Finally, The Sidmouth Brass Band.

The arrival of the Lifeboat, "Rimington", down the High Street.

The procession wended its way down Landpart (Temple Street), past Elysian Field where a handsome arch spanned the gateway. The entire roadway was hung with flags stretched over the road from house to house. The next stop was the Vicarage, where the grounds were decorated. The procession had to keep stopping, due to the height of the decoration which did not allow for the mast of the lifeboat to pass underneath. It continued through the crowds of sightseers in the High Street and Fore Street, again turned West along the Esplanade as far as Glen Road.

It then proceeded back along the Esplanade, past the York Hotel. It passed the site of the Lifeboat House, and going through the Volunteers who were in open order. The Boat was placed close to a platform attached to the grandstand erected for the comfort and convenience of the ladies of Sidmouth and its neighbourhood. There were 41 of them, more than the constructors calculated. The committee took their places on the part of the stand allocated to them. The crowd at this point numbered in thousands lining the road and the heights above the Alma Bridge.

At the command of the Inspector of Lifeboats, Captain Ward, the crew moved into the boat and lowered the mast and flags.

Silence was called for and Captain Ward spoke on behalf of the National Lifeboat Institution and of Mrs. Rimington, the benevolent lady who had presented the boat to the town of Sidmouth. The vicar of Sidmouth, the Rev. H. G. J. Clements, offered a prayer for the success of the boat. Mrs. Thornton then dashed the bottle against the stern, naming the boat the 'Rimington' and advising that 'God speed her'.

The craft was then pulled across the beach and into the sea. The boat behaved extremely well during the trial which lasted up to an hour, including being turned over to show her self-righting qualities.

The lifeboat was thirty-three feet long by eight foot six inches wide, with ten oars and taking a crew of thirteen. These included the Coxswain, Edward Bartlett, with assistant Coxswain James Ash, Bowman George Woolley. The rest of the crew were, William Barnard, William Baron, William Bartlett, Henry Conant, John Hayman. William Mortimer, Theophilus Mortimer, Isaac Perriam, John Richards and John Woodley. The crew, all local fishermen, had only a sail and oars to pull the boat through to rough seas on their life saving missions out into what became known as "Dead Man's Bay".

Launching the lifeboat.

The Rimington outside the boat house.1879.   Picture V. Bartlett.

The Sidmouth lifeboat had the distinction of being the only one in the country to have ever rescued a member of the royal family. It happened as H.M.S. Lively anchored in the bay so that the Duke of Edinburgh (Queen Victoria's second son) could land and inspect the coastguard station. The ships steam Pinnace was lowered to ferry the Duke and his party to shore. It nearly capsized in the south-easterly swell. The Rimington was launched and the party were transferred onto her.

LIFEBOATS AND RECORDS.

'Rimington'. The gift of Mrs. Rimington, of London. 1869 – 1895. 6 Launches, 32 Lives Saved.

1872	September 5th.	Brig 'Frederick William' of Guernsey.	8	Lives saved
	December 31st.	Bargue 'Emmeline' of Bordeaux.	11	
1877	August 7th.	Schooner 'Wave' of Guernsey.	6	
1878	March 29th.	Smack 'Lady of the Lake' of Portsmouth.	3	
1881	May.	H.M.S. Lively.		
1883	July 29th.	Schooner 'Hope' of Ryde.	4	

The William and Francis.

The William and Francis.

The Rimington was replaced with the 'William & Francis'. The gift of Miss Base, of Dalston. Built in 1885, order number 40, type SR, cost £345. Thirty-four feet long, ten-oared, self-righting lifeboat.

'William & Francis'

7 Launches, 6 Lives saved.

1887	December 9th.	Brig 'Albany', of Greenock.
1905	August 3rd.	3 Fishing Boats.
1906	November 21st.	Smack 'Julia' of Plymouth.
1910	November 27th.	Watching.
1911	July 29th.	Sailing dinghy and motor boat.
	December 6th.	Watching.
	December 7th.	Schooner 'Maria' of Geestemunde.

Lifeboat Boats Officers and Crews.

Coxswains

E. Barrett	September 1869.
H. Conant	1878.
G. Horn	October 1889 - November 1901.
R. Solomen	November 1901 - September 1912.

Second Coxswain

J. Ash	September 1869.
R. Solomen	November1890 - November1901.
J. F. Horn	November 1901 - September 1912.

Bowman

G. Woolley	1869.
F. Bartlett	April 1892 - November1901.
T. Woolley	November 1901 – March 1912

Crew members in September 1869; William Mortimer, Theophilus Mortimer, William Barnard, William Baron, Jim and William Bartlett, Henry Conant, Fred Farrant, John Woodley, John Richards and John Hayman.

Other later names found; Dan Hook and Banty Hook, Isaac Perriam, Jim Roach, S. Ware, Bob and George Woolley.

The Lifeboat House.

The stone above the side door.

The first Lifeboat House was completed for the Rimington in December 1869, on the west corner of Ham Lane and the Esplanade. The signal for calling the crew was by the firing of two rockets from the Rocket house in Alma Lane, where they were stored. The rocket house is now a very much-altered private house.

In 1912 the Lifeboat was withdrawn and the station was closed due to lack of use. The reason was that by then Exmouth had a powerful steam powered lifeboat.

Mr H Daniell, wrote in his Recollections of Sidmouth, that there used to be a splendid barometer kept in a niche inside the building. It had inscribed on either side of its calibrated face two jingles of weather lore;

> 'Long notice long last' 'Short notice soon past'
> 'First rise after low, Foretells stronger blow'.

The barometer was at one stage moved into the Ham shelter under the port-hole where it was wantonly damaged by senseless youth.

The life boathouse was kept and used as storage and garages.

All were demolished to make way for a large block of flats in 1991, called Trinity Court. Only the stone pediment from the side doorway, with the initials R.N.L.B.I. remain, having been built into the side-wall of the flats.

In May 1912 Mr. W. H. Hasting presided over a meeting in the Manor Small Hall to consider forming a swimming and life saving association. At a later meeting the Sidmouth Swimming and Life Saving Society was formed, and started with thirty nine members. In 1914 Mr. W. G. Wright was Secretary. Also in this year, the Lord of the Manor had kindly consented to have a portable bathing shelter on the foreshore. This proved a great boon to members. Members had also constructed a diving board.

By 1936 the membership stood at 84. They also had a Polo group who gave life saving classes. In 1919 there was a Sidmouth Lads' Swimming Club. They had a tent on the beach and a diving raft, but both were destroyed in a unexpected storm on August 28th 1919.

Sidmouth Life Saving Club, started in about 1968. This was a part time beach patrol at Jacobs Ladder beach. They had the use of a room in the Watch Tower, at the top of Jacobs Ladder.

President was the Revd. Donald Peyton-Jones, from Salcombe Regis. Captain, Keith Roberts, Secretary, Alan Phillips, Treasurer, Tony Cook. Later to be joined by David Hill, Robert Bennet and Peter Evans. In 1970 they had been lent an inflatable dinghy powered by an outboard motor.

The first Rescue Boat the Club bought was in about 1975. This was a second-hand hull, bought from Atlantic College, Rousdon, South Wales. A second-hand Evenrude engine was supplied by Exmouth Marine Services, Chief mechanic was Alan Meacham from Honiton. The Council then gave them the use of the boathouse at Port Royal.

They made a trailer for the boat from scaffold poles. Life saving teams represented Sidmouth at many South West and National Championships. The Sidmouth Sharks were formed for young people, boys and girls, who were keen on water sports. They met on Thursday nights while the seniors met on Fridays.

By 1982 with an increase in boating, the Sidmouth rescue service became available full time. From 1985 they were using a Rigid Inflatable Boat called 'Storm'. The next boat was 'Spirit of Sidmouth'. This had its own trailer and towing vehicle.

It became a registered charity, completely independent of the R N I L, and was called 'Sidmouth Inshore Rescue Service Trust'.

A new Inshore Rescue Centre was built on the east side of Ham lane. This in turn was badly damaged in a storm and had to be rebuilt. In 1998 an extension was built to the boat-house.

On March 10th 2005 the charity name changed to 'Sidmouth Lifeboat'.

On March 30th 1991 a new Atlantic Class rescue boat, 'Spirit of Sidmouth' was dedicated at a ceremony at the HQ building.

In 1999 Sidmouth Inshore Rescue Service got a new Atlantic 21 lifeboat, Coxswain Alan Stevenson, crew Simon Sparrow and Dennis Hutchings. This was a much larger seven-metre vessel, powered by two 60-horsepower water cooled outboard units. The launch tractor was a highly modified Renault agricultural tractor, which could go into the sea enabling the lifeboat to float off its trailer with its engine running.

On May 27th 2000, a dedication service was held at the lifeboat station for the new lifeboat. Lady Clinton named the boat "Sidmouth Herald".

In October 2004, after nineteen months of fund raising by the people of Sidmouth, spearheaded by Freddy Wedderburn, a new tailor-made lifeboat was built for the town by the firm, V. T. Halmatic, it was based on an Arctic 24 self-righting Rigid Inflatable inshore lifeboat, with a number of modifications. Cost £13,000. It is powered by two 2x 115 hp Mariner outboard motors, with a third as a back-up for emergencies. It is equipped with GPS navigation system, radar and sonar. As the lifeboat was bigger than the old one, alterations had to be made to the old trailer, and the building, to fit into their HQ. This new Lifeboat, had a new name, 'The Pride of Sidmouth'. Named by patron, Judi Spiers, on Saturday October 16th. 2004. Presented to the Senior Coxswain, Simon Sparrow and Second Coxawain, Rob Cooper. It carries a four-man crew.

In April 2006 a new tractor and trailer for the 'Pride of Sidmouth' was launched. The tractor. a modified Renault, rebuilt by Mr. Bowler, and a heavier trailer with a hydraulic system that can launch the lifeboat at any angle from the beach. Mike Vittles was the driver and Simon Sparrow, Senior coxswin, Perrry King helmsman.

Also the lifeboat had upgraded each engine from 115 hp to Mariner 135 hp.

"Pride of Sidmouth". Sidmouth's Independent Lifeboat. Photo by Simon Horn.

Full time lifeguards were appointed to look after the beaches at Sidmouth in 2001, and later had a hut on the beach at the western end of the Esplanade in the summer. This service is no longer in operation.

SHIPWRECKS

I have not researched the shipwrecks around the bay for this book, but a few accounts I have may be of interest to the reader.

1812. The Samuel. One of the coal barges, which landed coal onto the beach, was wrecked in 1812 in a storm.

In May 1815 near Ladram. It was not bad weather which caused this accident.
A newly married couple and friends were on their way back to Sidmouth by boat. One of the men lost his hat, and as he leaned over the side of the boat to retrieve it from the water, the boat capsized and all nine people were drowned.

1838. The Agnes was wrecked on the beach.

1872. The Margaret of Goole. off Salcombe.

1906. The Shamrock.
Extracts from the report in The Sidmouth Herald:
'On Wednesday 25th April 1906, great excitement was seen on the Esplanade. About three miles from shore, a Beer trawler The 'Shamrock' was on its way to Ladram Bay with a crew of two, Fred Driver aged 46 and William Bartlett aged 19. The sea was rough but not with sufficient force to cause alarm. Casual observers with glasses on the Esplanade noticed a fishing boat was sinking. Several small rowing boats, and one of the coast guard boats immediately put to sea.
Favoured by the wind blowing off the shore, the rescuers made good time to the scene. By now The Shamrock had sunk, leaving the two fishermen with only their oars to hold on to. They were also hampered by their heavy clothes while they waited for help. The boat that rescued the fishermen was manned by W. J. Smith, F. Smith and Hayman Salter.
With the wind and tide against them it took nearly two hours to get back to shore. The accident happened about 10.30 am. It was now 12.30 and hundreds of onlookers had gathered on the sea front. The coast guard boat made for the watch house while the boat containing the Beer men and the other boats came onto the beach in front of Fore Street..
As well as the coast guard boat the other boats that went to the rescue were manned by R. Wooley, T. Wooley, W. Farrant. J. Farrant and T. Bartlett.
A collection was made by Messrs Weeks and J. Farrant on the Esplanade immediately after the occurrence, and this amounted to £5. 2s. 0d. This was shared equally between the rescued and the rescuers.'

The Beer fishermen and their rescuers with their oars.

1911. The Maria.

In December in one of the worst storms, the sea smashing boats and heaping shingle over the sea front, the three-masted German schooner, Maria, was seen about ten miles off Sidmouth wallowing in mountainous seas. The rockets were fired and the lifeboat crew were immediately equipped and made ready for the off. The lifeboat, 'William & Francis,' was got over the slipway, but with the tide running out and the huge waves running up the beach the carriage wheels were sinking in the fine shingle. With great difficulty the crew and helpers, now all drenched with sea water, launched the lifeboat. With the sail set, the crew pulled seaward and it took two hours to reach the schooner with its captain and crew of six. They were now practically at the mercy of the waves. They were all saved. The weather was so bad that the lifeboat Coxswain, Mr. Soloman decided to lead the Maria and crew to Lyme Regis harbour for the night. The lifeboat could not return Sidmouth until the next day where hundreds of townspeople gathered to cheer the crew safely home.

1916. The Grindon Hall.

On Sunday November 5th. The Steamer Grindon Hall was driven ashore under the Salcombe Cliff in the fiercest of gales, having drifted eastwards out of control. Captain Brewis and the 15 crewmen were trying to shelter on the lee side of the deck as waves broke over the hull. The coastguard sent for a rocket to send a line to the ship, but decided to cross over the river with a small group of men and get nearer the ship. They edged their way as tight to the cliffs as they could, often drenched by high waves.

The line was too short so Billy Leo, the cobbler and hero of the day, with the rope tied around his waist swam out to the ship to start the rescue.

All the crew were rescued, and the only danger then was that she might break up on the shingle by the pounding from the sea. On Monday a tug came over from Exmouth, but for some days it was impracticable to do any thing but mend the hole in her hull. She was turned over to a salvage company. On November 24th, having fixed anchors out to sea she pulled herself off the shingle by her own steam windlasses. She steamed slowly west under the escort of tugs.

In August 1938, after a disastrous thunderstorm the river Sid was in was in full flood. Several persons were on the eastern side of the river bank by the sea shore. The mouth of the river was closed by a bank of shingle, and all but two people made their way back to the Alma bridge side, just as the shingle bank gave way and the river broke through in full flow. A lady and gentleman were cut off. Mr. A. Kibby launched a boat and rowed across the river and he managed to get both people into his boat. By now the volume of the backed up water took charge and swept then out to sea, capsizing and throwing all three into the sea. Dorien Squance and two fishermen. W. Harris and E. Smith pushed out boats to the rescue and all three were rescued.

In August 1974 the Liberal Party leader Jeremy Thorpe arrived in Sidmouth to make a speech at the Drill Hall, part of his tour around the westcountry by Hovercraft. There was a good sea running and nearly high tide. They managed to get part way onto the beach near the Bedford steps, and Mr. Thorpe landed. The hovercraft pulled back and went on round towards Port Royal, hoping for a better landing place. The waves were by now about six feet high, and the four man crew were in danger. Local trawler men John Govier, Stan Bagwell, Jeremy Thorpe and a policeman, joined in trying to secure the craft. They managed to attach a rope to the hovercraft and such was the struggle to hold her that the cleat holding the rope broke. A high wave hit the large propeller on the back of the hovercraft.

The engine cut out deflating the curtain and the beach made holes in the base. She was filling with water. The remaining crew got ashore and the rescue was at an end.

Politicians, it is said, always have an answer. Mr. Thorpe carried on with the meeting and said 'I am grateful to all who helped. Holding this meeting proves the Liberal Party operates equally well in fair weather and foul'. When the tide dropped the hovercraft was winched up on to the Esplanade, and was quite an attraction until she was taken away by road a few days later.

Jeremy Thorpe coming ashore. Picture Sidmouth Museum.

2007. The Napoli.

Saturday January 20th The MSC Napoli was making headline news.

The 62,000 ton cargo ship was holed in the heavy seas off The Lizard. She started to list and was at the mercy of the sea. A major rescue took place in the severe gale, helicopters lifted the 26 crew off the life raft from the tremendous seas.

It was then decided that the ship would be then taken under tow to Portland Harbour. However by the time she was off the coast of Branscombe the vessel was on the point of sinking. It was decided to ground her on a sand-bar, before losing her with her cargo of some 2,000 or more containers in deeper waters. In the very rough seas it was only hours before cargo was being washed up on the beaches. Hundreds of people started to collect 'souvenirs'. Branscombe was over-run by sightseers, wreckers, cars and vans. About 200 containers had been washed off the deck onto the beach and were very soon being smashed open by people out to get whatever was inside. Hundreds of new goods, wine barrels, motor bikes, spare parts for cars, perfume, shoes, the list could go on, were being taken off the beach.

Another major threat was the tons of fuel and engine oil, and toxic liquids on board the ship. Also the plastic, timber and cardboard etc. left by the looters and scavengers who had come down from all over the country leaving the beach covered in rubbish.

In some of the containers were personal properties, family items, furniture, and people sending goods and valuables home or abroad.
The beach, after a long delay, was finally closed and fenced off as was the whole of the village of Branscombe.

By the middle of the first week the weather changed, from the gales and very rough seas, to calm sea and fine weather, perfect for the salvage workers.
One of the first tasks was to pump the heavy fuel oil off the boat onto storage boats.
Boats began to arrive to start the clear up around the Napoli. Two boats started to locate about 47 sunken containers. Two massive cranes on the Rotterdam-based Bigfoot 1 barge were brought in to start lifting off all the remaining containers and load them, one at a time, on to boats to take them to Portland harbour.

Picture by Susan Willey LRPS.

Picture by Susan Willey LRPS.

There was more rough weather and the work stopped. The barge returned to Portland until the weather improved. More goods were washed off the ship and washed up onto the beach.

At the time of writing the salvage operations are ongoing. Reports say it could take a year to clear. Meanwhile Sidmouth can enjoy the extra trade from the continued interest of sightseers.

REFERENCES AND CREDITS

Vernon Bartlett's notes and writings.
Reverend Edmund Butcher. Writings.
Joyce Crabtree.
Harry S. Daniell's recollections of Sidmouth, Out to Beach.
John Govier.
E. Holland.
Peter & Rosemary Hook
Ivor Inches article in the Sidmouth Herald
Reg Lane's researches. Sidmouth Museum.
Life and Times in Sidmouth, by Julia Creeke.
T. H. Mogridge MD, Descriptive sketch of Sidmouth.
Peter Orlando Hutchinson, Notes. Sid Vale Association Newsletters.
Mr. and Mrs. Seward of the Kingswood Hotel.
Sidmouth Directory and Advertiser.
Sidmouth Museum.
Teach Yourself Books, Seamanship.
The First Week in August, by Derek Schofield.
The Sidmouth Herald.
The Sidmouth News.
The Sidmouth Volunteers 1914 - 1918, by John Tindall.
Garland Pickhard
Gordon Reed, Photographer.
Risdon's Survey of Devon.
Westcountry Studies Library, Exeter.

POSTCARDS

Art Co., Seaton.
B. & D. Ltd.
J. A. Bellinger.
E. G. Castle.
A. W. Ellis.
F. Frith.
G. T. Harris.
G. E. C. Postcards.
Lillywhite Ltd.
Photochrom Co.
The Regent.
Southwoods.
Valentine's Series.

PICTURES

J. Ankins.
H. Clapp.
A. Dean.
J. Edwards.
P. Flynn.
J. Govier.
E. Holland.
S. Horn.
Sidmouth Herald.
Sidmouth Museum.
Sidmouth Sailing Club.
G. Read.
P. Tully.
S. Willey.

Credits for front cover pictures

Engraved by J. Walker. July 1796.
From a drawing by W. Rowe.
Published by J. Ronson,
16 Rosomand Street, London.
Loaned by E. Holland.

Wallis's Library, 1818.
Shed and room for morning recreation.
Westcountry Studies Library, Exeter.

West view of Sidmouth, 1828.
Signed J. P. R.
Westcountry Studies Library, Exeter.

Credits for Back cover pictures

Jacobs Ladder Beach, late 1800s.

The Beacon Light, The Esplanade, early 1900s.

Alma Bridge, late 1855 - 1899.